Forty Years of World's Largest Democracy

A Survey of Indian Elections

Forty Years of World's Largest Democracy

A Survey of Indian Elections

G.N.S.Raghavan
and
G.Balachandran

Gian Publishing House
for
Press Trust of India

Gian Publishing House
4-C Ansari Road
Daryaganj, New Delhi 110002

ISBN 81-212-0332-5

PRINTED IN INDIA

Published by Mrs. Gayatri Garg for Gian Publishing House New Delhi 110002 for Press Trust of India New Delhi 110001.

Laser type set by Shiva Shakti Laser Printing Works 4B, Ansari Road, Daryaganj New Delhi 110002

Printed at Goyal Offset Printers, Delhi.

Contents

List of Tables

Foreword

When free India prepared in the winter of 1951-52 for its first general elections on the basis of universal adult franchise, many persons abroad--and quite a few Indians--wondered whether democracy would work successfully in a country with a low level of literacy and with diverse religions and languages.

The doubts have been disproved more than once over the last four decades. During this period, the people have on nine occasions chosen their representatives in the Lok Sabha (House of the People) of the Indian parliament. In the States, the electors have voted in and out of power various political parties of the Centre, the Left and the Right, and varied alliances of such.

Daniel Moynihan, a former ambassador of the U.S.A. to India, remarked: "Half of the people on earth who live in a society with civil liberties live in India." The fascinating story of the working of the world's largest democracy is told in the present work.

It provides factual data on electors, voters and the fortunes of all-India and regional political parties in the elections held during the last forty years. It also examines the issues which figured in the election manifestos and campaigning of the principal contending parties in the latest elections to the ninth Lok Sabha in November 1989. Many of these issues--ranging from poverty and illiteracy to communalism, corruption and electoral reform--are problems that the country will continue to have to cope with in the coming years.

Press Trust of India is happy to have sponsored this publication. Incorporated in the year of independence as the first wire news agency to be owned and run by Indian newspapers, PTI took over the operations of the Associated Press of India--a wholly owned subsidiary of Reuters--in February 1949. Since then, PTI has been telling the country and the world, hour after hour and day after day, the story of the triumphs and travails, the social and economic challenges and responses, of the democratic process in India.

I am thankful to the authors of the present work for undertaking it at my suggestion. G.N.S. Raghavan earlier wrote a history of the emergence and growth of PTI against the background of the origin and development of the Indian Press, under the title *PTI Story*. Dr. G. Balachandran is a versatile researcher who has made his mark as an election expert. He is known for his modification of the Cube Law model for election prognosis. The authors have drawn on PTI's extensive election coverage and computerised data with the help of Arun Kumar, PTI's Chief News Editor. However, any views expressed by them in the course of this basically factual and analytical work are their own.

I have no doubt that this book, filled with data and with significant information on 20th century India during the colonial and post-independence periods, will be found useful by students of current affairs, in the country and outside, in understanding the fast-moving developments in India's vibrant democracy.

P. UNNIKRISHNAN

General Manager
Press Trust of India
30 April 1990

Chapter 1

Five Hundred Million Electors

The year 1949 marked a turning point in the political history of the two most populous countries of the world. In China, the civil war ended with the victory of the Communist forces over the Kuomintang and the establishment of one-party dictatorship in the name of the proletariat. In India, which had become in August 1947 a self-governing Dominion of the British Commonwealth, the Constituent Assembly concluded its work. The Constitution of a sovereign democratic republic of India drafted by it came into effect on 26 January, 1950.

(i) Universal Adult Franchise

A notable feature of the new Constitution was that it provided adult franchise, for women equally with men. India's emergence as the world's largest democracy was dramatically evidenced by the first general elections held during the winter of 1951-52 for the Lok Sabha (House of the People), the directly elected House of the Indian Parliament, and for the State Assemblies.

The Election Commission of India is the authority vested, in terms of Article 324 of the Constitution, with the responsibility for "the superintendence, direction and control of the preparation of the electoral rolls for, and the conduct of, all elections to Parliament and to the Legislature of every State and of elections to the offices of President and Vice President". The Commission said in its report on the first general election that it was "a great experiment, unique in the world in its stupendousness and complexities. The carrying out of this unprecedented experiment attracted world-wide attention. In fact every country desiring to adopt parliamentary elections on adult franchise but faced with difficulties in the shape of illiteracy, ignorance and undeveloped communications, evinced the utmost interest in the Indian elections." The ballot system provided for the allotment of a pictorial symbol for identifying each contestant in a constituency. This was for the benefit of non-literate voters. The device was necessary because the level of literacy as ascertained at the 1951 Census was only 16.6%.

Never before in any country had nearly 81 million citizens cast their votes in free elections. It is remarkable that there was political participation on this scale, despite widespread illiteracy. The voter turn-out was 46.6% of the registered electors eligible to vote, who numbered a litle over 173 million. The proportion of the electorate who exercised their franchise has been higher in subsequent elections. It is now about 60% (See Table I). The size of the electorate has been rising at an accelerated rate along with the growth in population.

TABLE I

Men and women voters as % of the electors

Year	*Men*	*Women*	*Total*
1952	50,975,932 (53.51)	29,733,270 (38.15)	80,709,202 (46.6)
1957	55,924,441 (54.72)	35,405,424 (38.73)	91,329,865 (47.16)
1962	70,703,050 (62.05)	47,764,170 (46.63)	118,467,220 (54.75)
1967	86,460,463 (66.29)	66,264,048 (55.14)	152,724,511 (60.94)
1971	87,382,907 (60.9)	64,153,895 (49.12)	151,536,802 (55.29)
1977	109,609,940 (65.63)	84,653,975 (54.91)	194,263,915 (60.49)
1980	115,133,649 (62.16)	87,271,764 (51.22)	202,405,413 (56.92)
1984	134,122,952 (68.18)	107,123,935 (58.6)	241,246,887 (63.56)
1989	N.A.	N.A.	298,905,106 (59.94)

During the colonial period, frequent famines and epidemics used to take a heavy toll of life and kept the population growth rate low. There was actually a decline in the population of the territories now constituting India from 252 million at the 1911 Census to 251 million at the 1921 Census. Just a few years before the British quit India, there was a terrible famine in Bengal in 1943. The toll in the famine was a million and a half lives according to official estimates and, inclusive of deaths from the epidemics that raged in the wake of the famine, twice that figure according to non-official estimates. After independence there have been no large-scale deaths from starvation. This is because of increased food production, and the import of foodgrains whenever and to the extent necessary. It is a different matter that widespread poverty results in malnutrition and in mortality from diseases related thereto.

Deaths from communicable diseases have also been brought down through programmes for the eradication or control of what used to be mass killers, like malaria, cholera, smallpox and tuberculosis. The incidence of malaria alone used to be about 75 million cases per year, resulting in nearly 800,000 deaths annually. By 1965 the incidence of malaria came down to about 100,000 cases.

As a result, the expectation of life of the average Indian has gone up from about 32 years in 1951 to 54.4 years in 1980. With no comparable reduction in the birth rate despite a massively funded family planning programme, the population growth rate since independence has been high. Correspondingly, there has been a steep rise in the number of electors for the successive elections to the Lok Sabha. Figure 1 on page 4 depicts the size of the electorate in the nine elections from 1952 to 1989.

It is indicative of the importance attached by the Indian Government to the control of population growth that the Constitution was amended in 1976 so as to avoid a political disadvantage for States which promote family planning effectively. Article 81, dealing with the composition of the House of the People, provides that "there shall be allotted to each state a number of seats in the

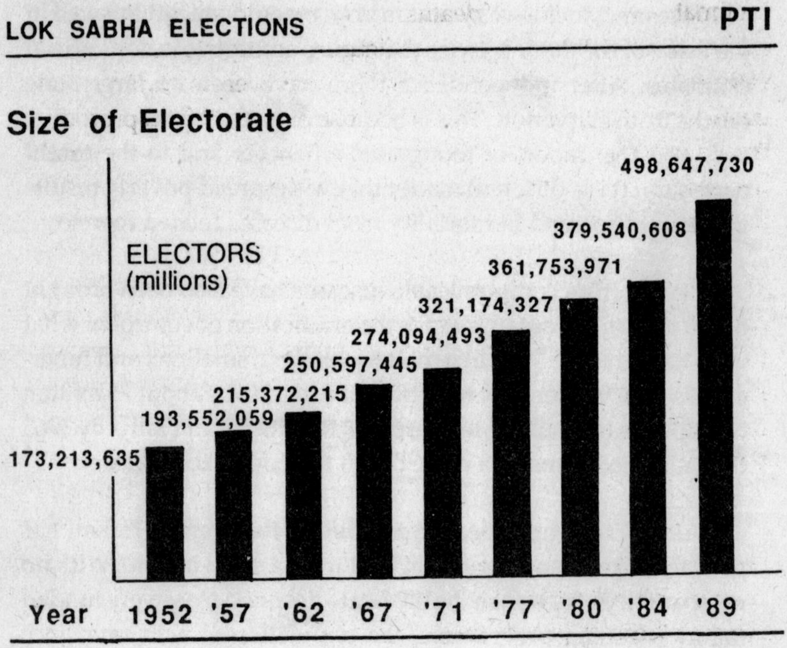
LOK SABHA ELECTIONS
PTI
Size of Electorate
ELECTORS
(millions)
173,213,635
193,552,059
215,372,215
250,597,445
274,094,493
321,174,327
361,753,971
379,540,608
498,647,730
Year
1952
'57
'62
'67
'71
'77
'80
'84
'89

Fig. 1

House of the People in such manner that the ratio between that number and the population of the State is, so far as practicable, the same for all States". Lest those States which pursue the family planning programme with vigour should have fewer representatives in the Lok Sabha compared to other States where the population growth rate is higher, the 42nd amendment of the Constitution, enacted in 1976, inserted the proviso that "the last preceding census of which the relevant figures have been published shall until the relevant figures for the first census taken after the year 2000 have been published, be construed as a reference to the 1971 Census."

(ii) Reduction in Voting Age

Article 326 of the 1950 Constitution, dealing with elections, initially read: "The elections to the House of the people and to the Legislative Assembly of every State shall be on the basis of adult suffrage; that is to say, every person who is a citizen of India and who is not less than twenty-one years of age on such date as may be fixed in that behalf by or under any law made by the appropriate legislature, and is not otherwise disqualified under this Constitution or any law made by the appropriate legislature on the ground of non-residence, unsoundness of mind, crime or corrupt or illegal practice, shall be entitled to be registered as a voter at any such election."

This article was amended during 1989, prior to the elections held in November of that year to the ninth Lok Sabha and to some State Assemblies, so as to lower the voting age to eighteen. This change enfranchised well above 30 million young persons. Together with the growth in population, it resulted in a steep rise in the size of the electorate. The figure stood at 498,647,730 exclusive of the electors in Assam. (That State did not go to the polls because of the need, first, to scrutinise the voters' list so as to exclude ineligible foreign immigrants from Bangladesh). Inclusive of Assam, the size of the Indian electorate is now in excess of 500 million.

(iii) Women's Participation

Women participated alongside men on an increasing scale in every round of the freedom struggle, beginning with the agitation against the partition of Bengal in 1905 and culminating in the Quit India Movement of 1942. The saintly personality of Mahatma Gandhi, who assumed the leadership of the national movement in 1919, was the single most important factor in overcoming the resistance of men of the middle and upper classes to their women-folk venturing outside domestic walls to take part in public life. In the words of Sucheta Kripalani (1908-74), a prominent figure in the freedom movement who served for some years after independence as Chief Minister of Uttar Pradesh, India's most populous State, "Gandhiji's personality was such that he inspired confidence not only in women but in the guardians of women--their husbands, fathers and brothers. The standard of conduct that he laid down for his work was so high. Therefore, when women came out and worked in the political field, their family members knew that they were quite safe, they were protected. Had Gandhiji's leadership been not there, such a large number of women would not have come."

Women's participation in the freedom movement led to the acceptance of equal rights without their having to wage a struggle for the franchise like their sisters in the West. Figure 2 shows the extent of women's participation in the successive elections to the Lok Sabha.

Literacy among women being considerably lower than among men, it is not surprising that the proportion of eligible women electors who exercised their franchise has been less than the corresponding figure for men. But the gap in the participation rate has been narrowing over the years. Table I gives the number of men and women who exercised their vote in the nine elections to the Lok Sabha and, in parentheses, the proportion of actual voters as per cent of the total number of electors eligible to vote.

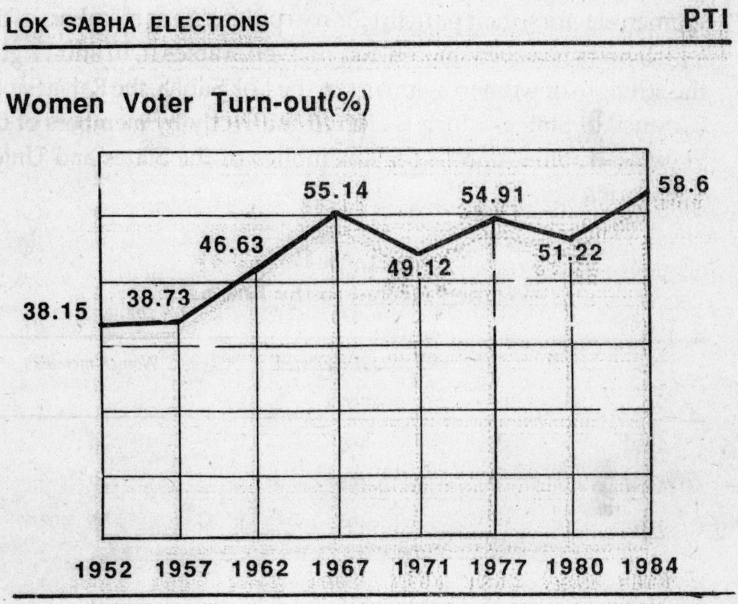
LOK SABHA ELECTIONS
PTI
Women Voter Turn-out(%)
38.15
38.73
46.63
55.14
49.12
54.91
51.22
58.6
1952
1957
1962
1967
1971
1977
1980
1984

Fig. 2

The absence of temporal regularity in the elections to the Lok Sabha is because, though the Constitution provides for the House of the People, and the State Assemblies, to be elected every five years, there have been premature dissolutions of legislatures, resulting in what are called 'mid-term' polls. The elections to the Lok Sabha due in 1976 were postponed, during the internal emergency, by one year.

In contrast to the upward trend in the exercise of the vote by women electors, their participation in public life as members of the legislatures has been limited and uneven. Tables II, III and IV give the strength of women members in the Lok Sabha, the Rajya Sabha (Council of States) which is elected indirectly by members of the State assemblies, and in the assemblies of the States and Union Territories.

TABLE II

Women elected to the Lok Sabha

Year	*Total of elected members*	*Women members*
1950	489	14
1957	494	27
1962	494	35
1967	520	31
1971	518	21
1977	542	19
1980	542	28
1984	528	42
1989	524	27

The proportion of women members in the Rajya Sabha (Council of States) with a total strength of 244 has been higher than in the Lok Sabha. The strength of women members shown in Table III includes women among the dozen members who are nominated by the President to the Rajya Sabha. Elections to the Rajya Sabha are biennial, since a third of the members retire on the expiration of every second year.

TABLE III

Women members of the Rajya Sabha

Date	*Number of women members*
24 October 1980	29
15 July 1982	23
4 February 1984	24
19 November 1986	28
1 May1990	26

Unlike the elections to the Lok Sabha which are normally held throughout the country at about the same time, elections to State assemblies take place at varying points of time.Table IV shows the number of men and women elected to State assemblies during different periods from 1970 to 1983.

TABLE IV

Women elected to State Assemblies

Period	*Total number elected*	*Men*	*Women*
1970-72	3264	3103	161
1974-75	901	874	27
1977	2671	2599	72
1978	1052	1022	30
1979-80	2590	2478	112
1982-83	1530	1486	44

The principle of equal rights for women having been affirmed during the freedom movement and guaranteed by the Constitution, the small proportion of women in the legislatures has not impeded legislation for improving the status and rights of Indian women.

In the Constituent Assembly there were only eleven women members out of the effective strength of 313 when the Assembly completed its work in November 1949. The under-representation of women did not stand in the way of the Constituent Assembly deciding to confer equal rights on women. Moreover, Clause 3 of Article 15 dealing with the Fundamental Right of Non-discrimination as between citizens reads: "Nothing in this Article shall prevent the State from making any special provision for women and children." This clause was inserted at the instance of B.N. Rau, constitutional advisor, who pointed out in a note on an early version of the present Article 15 that the wording as it then stood might affect adversely the establishment of separate schools, hospitals, etc. for women and children. This reflected the concern of members, irrespective of sex, for the vulnerable sections of society.

Of the nine Lok Sabhas elected so far, the first had the smallest number of women members. Yet it was that Lok Sabha which, along with the Rajya Sabha, enacted a series of measures in the mid-'fifties to reform and codify Hindu personal law so as to enforce monogamy, permit divorce on specified grounds, and give daughters and widows a share in succession to property.

During the freedom movement, women leaders were against reservation of seats for their sex in the central and provincial legislatures. They regarded reservation as a badge of weakness and backwardness, which they repudiated. They wanted women to prove their worth as equal competitors with men, and were confident that they would do so. A quarter century after independence, the Committee on the Status of Women (1971-74) rejected by majority a proposal for statutory reservation of seats for women in legislative bodies. The Committee said in its report, *Towards Equality:* "The women's cause in India has always been championed by all progressive elements, men as well as women. A climate favourable for the betterment of women's status can best be created by their joint efforts. Women's interests as such cannot be isolated from economic, social and political interests of groups, strata and classes of society. Though they have some real problems of their own, they share with men the problems of their groups, locality and community. Women have been competing as equals with men since 1952. They must continue to do so and stand on their own merits and intensify their political and social life. A departure from this equality will be a retrograde step."

However, the Committee on the Status of Women called upon political parties to "adopt a definite policy regarding the percentage of women candidates to be sponsored by them for elections to parliament and state assemblies. While they may initially start with 15%, this should be gradually increased so that in time to come the representation of women in the legislative bodies has some relationship to their position in the total population of the country or the State."

Chapter 2

Electoral System

(i) Divide and Rule: Separate Electorates

The Constitution of free India did away with the system of separate electorates based on religion, race and caste which had been devised by the British rulers in order to intensify divisions in Indian society and to weaken the national movement. The system based on separate electorates militated against a sense of nationhood by encouraging candidates to compete with each other in appealing to the separate identity and distinctive interests of voters belonging to one religion or race or caste.

Divide and rule was the fundamental basis of British imperial policy in India. During the anti-British uprising which swept across northern India in 1857, Hindus and Muslims had stood together at every level: among the sepoys recruited by the British for their army, the civilian population, as well as the princes and chieftains. It was desirable, therefore, from the viewpoint of the British rulers, to create a Hindu-Muslim cleavage, especially since some educated Hindus had begun to voice political aspirations. "We have maintained our power," said Sir Charles Wood, Secretary of State for India in the British government, in a communication to Lord Elgin, then Governor-General of India, in 1862, "by playing off one part against the other, and we must continue to do so. Do what you can, therefore, to prevent all having a common feeling. It obviously is a cardinal point in India to keep races and classes so far away from each other as to obviate as far as possible the danger of combined action. Do the ordinary work of the North-West Provinces with North-Western troops, Punjab ditto, and then have your Punjab troops ready to beat the Eastern with, and your Eastern troops ready to beat the Sikhs with, if occasion should arise. The natural antagonism of the races is no inconsiderable element of our strength. If all India was to unite against us, how long could we maintain ourselves?"

Separate electorates were created for Muslims under the Indian Councils Act of 1909. This was the first legislation which introduced the elective principle, though on an extremely limited scale and narrow franchise, in place of wholly nominated councils. The Government of India Act of 1919 extended separate electorates to the Sikhs in Punjab, Indian Christians in Madras Presidency, and to Anglo-Indians in Madras and Bengal. In the 'thirties the British rulers wanted to further extend the principle of separate electorates, beyond race and religion to caste, by creating such electorates for the then untouchable castes. Known initially as the Depressed Classes, they were significantly termed as Harijans or Children of God by Mahatma Gandhi who made it his life's mission to rid Hindu society of the blot of untouchability. The British Prime Minister Ramsay MacDonald announced on 16 August 1932 a 'Communal Award' under which there would be, in addition to general constituencies in which the Depressed Classes would vote along with other members of the Hindu community, 71 "special seats filled from Depressed Class electorates in the areas where these voters chiefly prevail."

(ii) Reservation of Seats

Gandhiji was not happy about the reservation of seats for Harijans, since caste Hindus might feel absolved of the moral responsibility of striving for the uplift of the untouchables; but if the latter wanted reservation, he said, he would not oppose it. But he was wholly against separate electorates for Harijans, and launched on an indefinite fast in protest. In the words of Prof. Ravinder Kumar,

"The position of the untouchables was radically different from that of the Muslims. Unlike the latter, the untouchables constituted an organic part of Hindu society, howsoever lowly be the position which they occupied within it. To confer upon them the dubious privilege of separate electorates was to condemn them for ever to the status of untouchables." Mediators eventually worked out an accord with Dr. B.R. Ambedkar, the Depressed Classes leader, and Gandhiji terminated the fast. Under the agreement, the untouchable voters in the reserved seats would, in the first instance, elect for each seat a panel of three or four candidates; the panel would then be put before the untouchable and caste Hindu voters for their joint choice. The Communal Award was modified accordingly by the British, and incorporated in the Government of India Act of 1935.

The Constitution of free India retained the system of reserving a certain number of seats for candidates belonging to the Scheduled Castes, as the Depressed Classes came to be known after they were listed in a schedule to the 1935 Act. Seats are reserved also for the Scheduled Tribes. In both cases, the voting is by joint electorates of all eligible voters in a reserved constituency. Article 334 provided initially that the reservations would be for a period of ten years. But this Article has been amended from time to time to extend the period, and the reservations will now continue till the year 2000.

As regards the quantum of reserved seats, the Constitution provides that the number of reserved seats both in the Lok Sabha and the State assemblies shall bear the same proportion to the total number of seats allotted to a State or Union Territory in the Lok Sabha, and the total number of seats in the Assembly, as the proportion of S.C./S.T. bears to the total population of the State or Union Territory. Since S.C. and S.T. candidates can contest non-reserved seats also, the constitutional provisions ensure that the proportion of seats held by Harijan and tribal members of the Lok Sabha and State assemblies is never below, but can exceed, their proportion in the total population.

Though the Constitution provides for reserved seats on the basis of joint electorates for S.C. and S.T. only, in effect considerations of caste (other than S.C.) play a dominant part in the political parties' choice of candidates in a vary large number of constituencies. The candidates of rival parties often belong to the same locally influential caste, or to competing coalitions of castes. Similarly, though there is no formal reservation of any constituencies for religious minorities, there are several constituencies with a concentration of Muslims or Christians in which the candidates of rival political parties are almost invariably Muslims or Christians. In Kerala, for example, the Lok Sabha constituency of Manjeri has always returned Muslim candidates, while no non-Christian has been elected from Muvattupuzha.

There is provision in the Constitution for the nomination of not more than two Anglo-Indians to the Lok Sabha by the President "if he is of opinion that the Anglo-Indian community is not adequately represented in the House of the People." Similarly, the Governor of a State may nominate one member of the Anglo-Indian community if he is of opinion that the "community needs representation in the Legislative Assembly of the State and is not adequately represented therein."

(iii) Anomalies of First-Past-the-Post

India retained after independence the system of single-member constituencies. It was introduced by the British when they conceded the nationalist demand for elected instead of wholly nominated legislatures, though the elections were held on severely limited franchise. Under this system, a candidate who gets first past the wining-post becomes the sole representative of a territorial constituency, even if he secures much less than half of the total vote. Political parties, likewise, can secure a huge majority of seats in a legislature with a minority of the popular vote.

The very first elections to the Lok Sabha, held in 1951-52, revealed the anomalies of the system of first-past-the-post. The

Indian National Congress secured 45.0% of the popular vote, but as many as 74.4% of the seats in the Lok Sabha. In none of the nine elections held so far to the Lok Sabha did the Congress party secure a majority of the popular vote, but it won a majority of the seats and formed the government on seven occasions. Similarly, the Janata Party secured a majority of seats with only 41.3% of the votes in 1977 and formed the government, while the Janata Dal, principal constituent of the National Front which formed the government in 1989, won a disproportionately high share of seats relative to votes. Figure 3 presents the percentage of votes and of seats secured by the winning party in the successive elections to the Lok Sabha.

The anomalies of the electoral system of first-past-the-post are further illustrated by Table V which presents data on the percentage of votes and of seats secured by the four front-running parties in the elections to the Lok Sabha. It will be seen that in 1967, securing only 40.8% of the popular vote, the Congress won 54.42% of the seats in the Lok Sabha and went on to form the government. In contrast, the Congress (I) in 1989 secured 39.33% of the popular vote, merely 1.47 percentage points less than in 1967, but only 37.02% of the seats. The drop in the Congress share of Lok Sabha seats was by as much as 17.40% percentage points. A non-fragmented opposition made all the difference to the fortunes of the Congress (I).

On the other hand in 1984, a fragmented opposition made a gift of the Moradabad seat to the Congress (I). Hafiz Siddique secured only 29.4% of the popular vote but was declared elected to the Lok Sabha from Moradabad. This was because of the division of votes between his two major opponents, belonging to the Lok Dal and the Bharatiya Janata Party. They got 27.6% and 21.0% of the votes, adding up to much more than the Congress share, but to no avail.

In the elections to State Assemblies, too, there has been a similar distortion of the vote-seat ratio as a result of the system of

LOK SABHA ELECTIONS PTI

Votes & Seats of the Ruling Party (%)

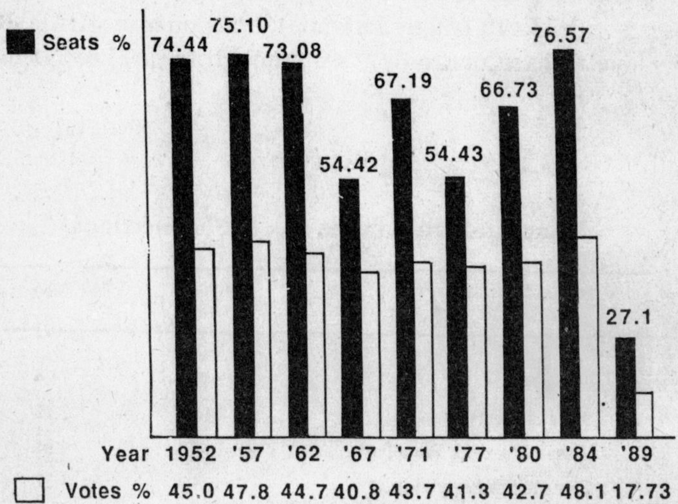

Figures relate to Congress except in 1977 (Janata) and 1989 (Janata Dal).

Fig. 3

first-past-the-post. Two examples may be cited. In Bihar, the Congress won a substantial majority of seats in the State Assembly and was able to form the government with 41.4% of the vote in 1952; 42.1% in 1957; 41.4% in 1962; 33.1% in 1972; 34.2% in 1980; and 39.3% in 1985.

In Tamil Nadu, in the 1984 elections to the State Assembly the All India Anna Dravida Munnetra Kazhagam (AIADMK) won 133 seats -- a majority -- with 37.1% of the vote and formed the government, while the Dravida Munnetra Kazhagam (DMK) with 29.5% of the votes got only 24 seats. In the elections held in January 1989, on the other hand, the situation was reversed. The DMK won 151 seats with 33.44% of the vote while the faction of the AIADMK led by Jayalalitha secured only 27 seats though it won 21.68% of the vote.

TABLE V

Principal Parties in the Lok Sabha Elections

Year of election	*Name of political party*	*% of votes*	*% of seats*
1952	Congress	45.0	74.4
	Socialist Party	10.6	2.45
	Kissan Mazdoor Praja Party	5.8	1.84
	Communist Party of India	3.3	3.27
	Other parties and Independents	35.3	17.99
1957	Congress	47.8	75.1
	Praja Socialist Party	10.4	3.84
	Communist Party of India	8.9	5.46
	Bharatiya Jan Sangh	5.9	0.8
	Others	27	14.77
1962	Congress	44.77	73.07
	Communist Party of India	9.9	5.87

Year of election	*Name of political party*	*% of votes*	*% of seats*
	Swatantra	7.9	3.64
	Praja Socialist Party	6.8	2.42
	Others	30.7	14.97
1967	Congress	40.8	54.42
	Bharatiya Jan Sangh	9.4	6.73
	Swatantra	8.7	8.46
	Communist Party of India	5.0	4.42
	Others	36.1	25.96
1971	Congress (Indira Gandhi)	43.7	66.02
	Congress (Organisation)	10.4	2.95
	Bharatiya Jan Sangh	7.4	4.24
	Communist Party (Marxist)	5.1	4.82
	Others	33.4	21.81
1977	Bharatiya Lok Dal (Janata Party)	41.3	54.42
	Congress (I)	34.5	28.41
	Communist Party (Marxist)	4.3	4.05
	Communist Party of India	2.8	1.29
	Others	17.1	11.8
1980	Congress (I)	42.7	66.72
	Janata Party	19.0	5.86
	Janata Party (Secular)	9.4	7.75
	Communist Party (Marxist)	6.1	6.80
	Others	22.8	12.85
1984	Congress (I)	48.1	76.56
	Bharatiya Janata Party	7.4	0.36
	Janata Party	6.7	1.84
	Communist Party (Marxist)	5.7	4.05
	Others	32.1	17.15

Year of election	Name of political party	% of votes	% of seats
1989	Congress (I)	39.33	37.02
	Janata Dal	17.73	27.1
	Bharatiya Janata Party	11.56	16.4
	Communist Party (Marxist)	6.32	6.1

(iv) Voters' Capacity for Judgement

The single-member territorial constituency system thus tends to exaggerate a swing away from or in favour of a political party. Nevertheless, the results of the successive elections to the Lok Sabha and the State Assemblies have shown the Indian voters' capacity to judge the performance of a party.

They removed the Congress from power at the centre for the first time in 1977, turned to it again in 1980, and once again rejected the Congress in 1989. At the State level the changes have been more extensive and frequent: from the Congress to a non-Congress party, and from one non-Congress party or alliance to another. It is also noteworthy that the bulk of the votes have been cast for candidates contesting on behalf of organised political parties rather for Independents.

The successful working of full-fledged multi-party democracy in India over the four decades since the coming into force of the republican Constitution doubtless owes to the fact that it was preceded by a hundred years of political organisation and activity. The first stirrings of political consciousness among the English-educated classes resulted in the formation of regional associations in the 1850's in the three Presidency capitals of Calcutta, Bombay and Madras. They urged steps towards representative government and sent petitions to the British Parliament asking for a less expensive and more responsive administration in India. Outside the coastal cities, too, there were organisations such as the Society for the Promotion of National Feeling started by Rajnarain Bose at

Midnapore in Bengal, the Sarvajanik Sabha of Poona formed in 1870, and district branches of the Mahajana Sabha of Madras which had its office room in the premises of the *The Hindu.*

An all-India political forum emerged with the formation of the Indian National Congress in 1885. It was the outcome of parallel efforts by Surendranath Banerjea (1848-1925), the first nationalist to achieve all-India influence, and by Allan Octavian Hume, a retired official of the British Indian administration. Banerjea belonged to a group of the Bengali intelligentsia who, as he put it, entertained "the conception of a united India, derived from the inspiration of Mazzini". He convened in December 1883 in Calcutta the first all-India conference of the politically conscious among English-educated Indians. The conference was attended by more than a hundred delegates from different parts of the country. The formation of an all-India forum of educated Indians was canvassed also by Hume, who had come to India in 1849 and served as a member of the Civil Service in various districts of the North West Provinces (including the area later to be known as the United provinces of Agra and Oudh and subsequently as Uttar Pradesh). Having been a witness to the 1857 Uprising, Hume felt the need for a channel of communication between the alien rulers and the ruled. He proposed, on his retirement from service, the formation of an association that would, in his own words, serve as "a safety valve for the escape of great and growing forces". Established in 1885, what was intended by Hume as a safety valve became over the years a spring of national renewal and under Gandhiji's leadership, of anti-imperialist mass mobilisation without resort to violence.

The Congress as well as non-Congress political parties fought elections to the Central Assembly and the provincial legislative councils held in the pre-independence period on narrow franchise. They formed, in the provinces, popular ministries with limited powers. This experience of legislative work and the exercise of executive power was of value to the political parties in operating democratic institutions after the Constitution of free India came into force.

Chapter 3

Growth of a Complex Polity

A country of sub-continental size, with diversities of language, religion and ethnicity comparable only to those of the Soviet Union, India had no multi-party democratic model to follow. Over the last four decades, a complex polity has evolved in India through such structural changes as the linguistic reorganisation of States and numerous amendments of the Constitution both to confer regional autonomy and to strengthen national integrity. The country has coped, by and large successfully, with the kind of strains and stresses that have surfaced in the Soviet Union in recent years after the iron lid of Stalinism was lifted.

(i) Political Parties and Alliances

The Congress party led by Jawaharlal Nehru won a big majority in the House of the People in the first elections held in 1951-52. But as the first Prime Minister, Nehru sought the widest cooperation in the building of a new India. Though he had earlier been derisive of Liberals who adhered to constitutional methods and did not participate in the civil disobedience movements, once independence was achieved he did not hesitate to seek their cooperation. The governments headed by Nehru were not party outfits confined to Congressmen but, to the extent that others would respond, they were governments of national talent. The successive governments included Dr. Shyama Prasad Mookerji, the distinguished educationist active in public life; persons with wide administrative experience like N. Gopalaswami Aiyangar and V.T. Krishnamachari; and subject-matter experts like B.R. Ambedkar, John Mathai, C.D. Deshmukh and T.T. Krishnamachari.

Nehru commended to the Chief Ministers of States a similar approach of seeking broad-based cooperation. In a letter of 16 August 1948, he referred to the Reserve Bank (Transfer to Public Ownership) Bill and said: "But more important than any particular legislative measure is the problem of how to deal effectively with the economic situation as a whole. In this matter we are at present trying to consult important interests and experts. I am glad to inform you that we are consulting even those who are normally completely opposed to Government. We do not wish to proceed in this and other matters on a narrow basis. Even if we are right in our policy but fail to win over large sections, our rightness will not take us very far. I would commend to you this example of attempting to win the cooperation of others."

Jawaharlal Nehru likewise sought the co-operation of the Left. No constructive response was to be expected at that time from the Communists. Founded in 1925, the Communist Party of India functioned during the inter-war years as part of a movement directed centrally by the Communist International (Comintern) based in Moscow. After Hitler's attack on the Soviet Union the Communists held that World War II which they had earlier described as an imperialist war had been transformed overnight into a people's war. They alienated themselves from nationalists by their opposition to the anti-British Quit India struggle launched in 1942. After the war, they swung to the other extreme and refused, till the early 'fifties, to acknowledge that India became politically independent in August 1947.

Even the non-Communist Left chose to keep aloof. The Congress Socialist Party, formed in 1934, used to function as a group within the Indian National Congress, and held its conferences alongside the annual sessions of the Congress. But the Socialists decided in 1948 to leave the parent body, thinking that they could offer an alternative to the Congress. How much they over-rated their influence was to be demonstrated soon. Acharya Narendra Dev and twelve other Socialist members resigned from the United Provinces Assembly to which they had been elected in 1946 on the Congress ticket. They could win none of the seats in the bye-elections that followed.

The exit of the Socialists weakened Jawaharlal Nehru in relation to conservative elements within the Congress. After Purushottamdas Tandon was elected as Congress President in September 1950, defeating J.B. Kripalani whom Jawaharlal Nehru preferred, Kripalani, Rafi Ahmad Kidwai and some others left the Congress in May 1951 to form the Kissan Mazdoor Praja Party. When Tandon subsequently resigned and Jawaharlal Nehru was elected as the new Congress President, he at once invited the colleagues who had broken away to return to the Congress. He explained in a letter of 27 September 1951 to Sri Krishna Sinha, Chief Minister of Bihar: "I am trying to build up something big and want every kind of person to help it." Kidwai responded to the invitation and rejoined the Congress, but Kripalani and many others did not. Soon after the general elections of 1951-52, the Socialists merged with the K.M.P.P. to form the Praja Socialist Party.

Though the Congress swept the polls both to the Lok Sabha and the State Assemblies, Nehru sought the cooperation of Jaya Prakash Narayan, leader of the P.S.P., in whom he saw a future Prime Minister. Nehru invited Narayan and his colleagues to join the Congress governments at the Centre and in those states where the P.S.P. was strong. But the talks failed because Jaya Prakash Narayan insisted on the prior acceptance of a minimum programme of radical reforms as the basis for cooperation. He said in the course of a letter of 4 March 1953 to Jawaharlal Nehru: "The proposal that you made to me was a bold and unusual one because the Congress party stood in no need of a coalition either at the Centre or in most of the States. But you rose above partisan considerations and took a statesmanlike step. What you proposed was, to my mind, not a parliamentary coalition in the accepted sense of the term, but a joint effort to build a new India. We are not a power in the legislatures, but we do claim to have a following in the country and a cadre which in some respects is superior to that of the Congress. A great deal would depend on how you conceived your own move in asking our cooperation. If it means only that a few of us are to be added to your cabinet and some of the State cabinets to strengthen the government and your hands in carrying out your present policies, the attempt would not be worth making. But if it means launching upon a bold, joint venture of national reconstruction, it might well have become a historic move. It is in this perspective that the draft programme was prepared."

In the words of Kamaladevi Chattopadhyaya (1903-88), who was a prominent Congress Socialist, "There were disinterested persons who asked Jaya Prakash to accept the invitation and, after strengthening his position, to try to implement his other demands, but he declined. So the opportunity was never given a trial. It is very difficult to say what course Indian politics would have taken, had Jaya Prakash accepted Nehru's offer." As it happened, by 1955 Jawaharlal Nehru persuaded the Indian Parliament and the Congress party to adopt resolutions proclaiming a socialistic pattern of of society as the objective which the country should strive for.

If the Congress and the Socialists could not join hands, neither could the Communists and the Socialists. When the Congress Socialist Party was formed, Indian Communists were following the sectarian line laid down in 1928 by the 6th Congress of the Comintern. They regarded the C.S.P. as 'a Left manoeuvre of the bourgeoisie' and as 'social fascists'. In 1935 the 7the Congress of the Comintern advocated the strategy of forming united fronts. Following this the Communist Party of India--which was then an illegal organisation--began to function through the C.S.P. from the time of the Lucknow Congress of 1936. When the Communist tactics of infiltration became known, the C.S.P. banned the further admission of Communists and later, at the Ramgarh session in 1940, decided on their wholesale expulsion.

The rift between the Socialists and the Communists worsened during the Quit India struggle which broke out in August 1942 and in which the Socialists took a prominent part. In the post-war years, the Socialists denounced Soviet actions in Eastern Europe and totalitarianism within the Communist countries. Communists, on the other hand, echoed the then line of Moscow and Peking which denounced Gandhism and branded Jawaharlal Nehru as a running dog of Anglo-American imperialism.

Within the Socialist movement there was a split in 1955 when Dr. Rammanohar Lohia broke away from the P.S.P. and formed a separate Socialist Party. The two Socialist parties contested the 1957 and 1962 elections separately. There was a merger of the two into the Samyukta (United) Socialist Party on 7 June 1964, only for the two wings to separate again on 31 January 1965 into the old P.S.P. and the S.S.P. comprising Lohiaites. The two once again contested the elections separately in 1967. They reunited on 9 August 1971, though splinter groups emerged in some states.

Following the Sino-Soviet rift and the hostilities of 1962 between India and China, the Indian Communist movement, too, suffered a split. In 1964 a new CPI (Marxist) was formed which was inclined towards Marxism as interpreted by the Chinese Communist leader Mao Tse-tung rather than by the Soviet leadership.

Two post-independence political formations emerged during the 'fifties and the 'sixties. The first was the Bharatiya Jan Sangh (now the Bharatiya Janata Party). It was founded in 1951 on the eve of the first general elections by Dr. Shyama Prasad Mookerji. He had resigned from the Indian Cabinet in protest against what he regarded as Prime Minister Nehru's weak handling of problems with Pakistan, in particular the forced exodus of large numbers of Hindus from Pakistan's eastern wing (now Bangladesh).

Dr. Mookerji wanted to promote a political party as an alternative to the Congress, but it was to be a nationalist and not a Hindu-communal alternative. This was in accordance with a resolution on the separation of religion, race and caste from politics which the Constituent Assembly of India had adopted on 3 April 1948 in the following terms: "Whereas it is essential for the proper functioning of democracy and the growth of national unity and solidarity that communalism should be eliminated from Indian life, this Assembly is of the opinion that no communal organisation which by its constitution or exercise of discretionary power vested in any of its officers or organs, admits or excludes from its membership persons on the ground of religion, race or caste or any of them, should be permitted to engage in any of the activities other than those essential for the bona fide religious, cultural, social and educational needs of the community, and that all steps, legislative and administrative, necessary to prevent such activities should be taken."

Shyama Prasad Mookerji had been closely associated with the Akhil Bharatiya Hindu Mahasabha. He tried to persuade the organisation to throw its membership open to all Indians, but failed in his attempt. It was for this reason that he felt the need to establish a new party. (The Hindu Mahasabha, like the Muslim League and the Akali Dal continued to function as a political body and contested successive elections--the resolution of the Constituent Assembly having remained unimplemented to this day.) The Jan Sangh stood for a strong and united India, including full integration of Jammu & Kashmir with the Indian Union. It asked for abrogation of Article 370 of the Constitution which accorded a special status to J & K. Dr. Mookerji died in 1953 while in detention in J & K, where he had been arrested when he was conducting an agitation against Article 370.

The Swatantra Party was formed in 1959 on a conservative economic plank. It had among its leaders some stalwarts of the freedom struggle: C. Rajagopalachari, a southern lieutenant of Mahatma Gandhi and the first Indian (and the last) Governor General of India as a Dominion of the British Commonwealth; Prof. N.G. Ranga, the peasant leader of the coastal Andhra region; and M.R. Masani, a former Congress Socialist who was among the earliest to question, like Milovan Djilas of Yugoslavia, the Marxist notion of one-party communist dictatorship in the name of the proletariat and to reconsider socialism understood as pervasive state ownership and control. Rajaji conducted a campaign through his speeches and writings against what he called 'control-licence-permit raj'.

Since dispossessed princes and big landlords, and industrialists associated with the Forum of Free Enterprise, backed Swatantra, it was widely perceived as a party standing for privilege. It was able to secure a significant share of the popular vote only in the feudal belt and in areas where its leaders like Rajaji and Ranga commanded local support. The Swatantra Party contested the elections of 1962, 1967 and 1971 but faded out thereafter.

The BJS, on the other hand, gradually grew in strength. Winning 3.1% of the votes in the 1952 elections to the Lok Sabha in which it secured three seats, it won 5.9% of the votes (and four seats) in 1957; 6.4% of the votes (and 14 seats) in 1962; and 9.4% of the votes (and 35 seats) in 1967.

The Jan Sangh figured in the controversy surrounding a major split in the Congress party in 1969. The split occurred following Prime Minister Indira Gandhi's withdrawal of her support to the Congress candidate for Presidentship of the Indian Union, N. Sanjiva Reddy. Switching her support to an independent candidate, V.V. Giri, Indira Gandhi asked her followers in the Congress to vote in the Presidential election according to their conscience. A major reason advanced by her for this change of position was that a syndicate of provincial Congress leaders, who she said were opposed to her progressive policies, had made overtures to the Jan Sangh for securing in favour of N. Sanjiva Reddy the votes of its legislators in parliament and the State legislatures.

Mrs. Gandhi's wing of the party, which eventually came to be known as the Congress (Indira Gandhi) or Congress (I) for short, won the 1971 elections to the Lok Sabha on a plank of 'Garibi Hatao' ('Banish Poverty'). Within a few years, however, there were agitations in some parts of the country, especially in Bihar and Gujarat, on the issues of rise in prices and of alleged corruption in the government. Against this background came the judgement in an election petition, adverse to Prime Minister Indira Gandhi, by a single judge of the Allahabad High Court. An internal emergency was proclaimed in 1975. For 18 months the Fundamental Rights stood suspended and the Press was placed under rigid censorship. In the absence of a free flow of information, there were widespread rumours of excesses committed during the emergency, especially of coercive steps in the northern States to enforce family planning.

The Congress party was displaced from power for the first time at the Centre early in 1977 as the result of the elections to the sixth Lok Sabha after the internal emergency. A new government headed by Morarji Desai was formed by the Janata Party--an alliance of the Congress (Organisation), the Bharatiya Lok Dal comprising ex-Congressmen many of whom had been imprisoned during the emergency, the Socialists, the Bharatiya Jan Sangh, and former supporters of Indira Gandhi such as Jagjiwan Ram who had become disillusioned with her leadership.

Soon, however, there were cracks in the alliance which called itself the Janata Party. A section of its leaders mounted a campaign against the dual membership of some Jan Sangh adherents in the Rashtriya Swayamsevak Sangh, an organisation that stands for Hindu consolidation and is opposed to proselytising activity by Christian and Muslim organisations. As in 1969, again in the late 'seventies the Jan Sangh became a factor in a split in the party in power at the Centre.

Charan Singh, Raj Narain and several others broke away and formed a new party, the Janata (Secular) which later converted itself into the Lok Dal. The Morarji Desai government lost its majority in the Lok Sabha, and a new government headed by Charan Singh was formed in mid-1979. But this government could not face the Lok Sabha since it lacked a majority, and fresh elections were held in January 1980 to form the seventh Lok Sabha. The Congress (I) was voted back to power. This was widely seen as the desire of voters to have a stable government at the Centre rather than an unstable combination of competing aspirants for office. After the 1980 elections the Jan Sangh left the Janata Party led by Chandra Shekhar and began functioning as the Bharatiya Janata Party.

In June 1980 the second son of Prime Minister Indira Gandhi, Sanjay Gandhi, who had been playing a leading part in public life since the days of the emergency, died in an aircrash. His brother Rajiv Gandhi, then a pilot in Indian Airlines, was persuaded by his mother to join politics. He was elected to the Lok Sabha from Sanjay Gandhi's constituency of Amethi in Uttar Pradesh and became Congress general secretary. When Indira Gandhi was assassinated on 31 October 1984, Rajiv Gandhi was sworn in by the President as Prime Minister. He also succeeded his mother as Congress president. Quickly calling the elections that were due for the eighth Lok Sabha, Rajiv Gandhi led the Congress (I) to a big victory in December 1989 on the crest of what was seen as a sympathy wave.

Vishwanath Pratap Singh was made Finance Minister by Rajiv Gandhi in the Cabinet formed by him following the elections. Belonging to a former princely family of Manda in Uttar Pradesh, V.P. Singh was elected to the U.P. Assembly in 1967 and stood by Indira Gandhi during the Congress split of 1969. Elected to the Lok Sabha in 1971, he served as Union Deputy Minister and subsequently as Minister of State in the Commerce Ministry from 1974 to 1977 (including the period of the emergency). Though re-elected to the Lok Sabha in January 1980, he was made Chief Minister of

Uttar Pradesh in June 1980. When an anti-dacoity operation launched by him did not succeed, V.P. Singh did something unusual for a politician in power. He resigned his chief ministership, in June 1982. Appointed as Union Minister of Commerce in January 1983, he was elected to the Rajya Sabha in July of that year.

As Finance Minister in the Rajiv Gandhi Cabinet, V.P. Singh launched a campaign against those--even if they belonged to big and politically influential business houses--who violated economic legislation. He was shifted to the Defence Ministry on 24 January 1987 but had to resign after he launched investigations into some controversial defence purchases. In July 1987 the Congress (I) expelled him from the party. He became the rallying point for a variety of persons critical of the functioning of the Congress (I) under Rajiv Gandhi's leadership. These included Arif Mohammed Khan who resigned from the Union government in 1986 on an issue of principle when the Muslim Women's Act was passed in response to demands made by male chauvinist leaders of the Muslim community. The Act exempted the Muslim husband from the duty, enjoined on Indian citizens by the Criminal Procedure Code as interpreted by the Supreme Court in 1985, of paying maintenance to a divorced wife if she should be in need of financial support. There were others who were dissatisfied with the positions they were given, or not given, by Rajiv Gandhi as Prime Minister and Congress president.

V.P. Singh formed on 2 October 1987 (Gandhiji's birth anniversary) the Jan Morcha, describing it as a people's movement rather than a political party. In June 1988 he was elected to the Lok Sabha as an Independent candidate from the Allahabad constituency, defeating his principal Congress (I) rival. Within a year V.P. Singh became the nucleus of a new political party, the Janata Dal. It was formed by the merger of the Jan Morcha, the Janata Party (including the Socialists), and the two wings of the Lok Dal led respectively by Devi Lal, then Chief Minister of Haryana and Ajit Singh, son of Charan Singh, founder of the Lok Dal.

A broader National Front was soon forged by V.P. Singh with a view to contesting the elections that were due to be held in about a year's time for the ninth Lok Sabha. Formally launched in Madras on 17 September 1988, the National Front included three powerful regional parties: the Dravida Munnetra Kazhagam which is in power in Tamil Nadu; the Telugu Desam Party founded by N.T. Rama Rao which ruled Andhra Pradesh at that time; and the Asom Gana Parishad which is in power in Assam. A fifth constituent was the Indian Congress (Secular).

(ii) Emergence of Regional Parties

The oldest of the three regional parties which became allies of the Janata Dal in the National Front is the Dravida Munnetra Kazhagam ('Organisation for progress of the Dravidians') of Tamil Nadu. It marked the transformation into a political party, in the year of independence, of the movement for social equality and self-respect that had been led since 1926 by E.V. Ramaswami Naicker, an aggressive atheist. This social movement was directed against the dominance of Brahmins not only in the social hierarchy of caste but in English education and consequently in the civil services and the modern professions. Since Brahmins were equated in popular ethnology--not altogether wrongly but in disregard of the racial mixing that has occurred over the centuries--with the Aryans who came originally as invaders from the north, the movement launched by E.V. Ramaswami Naicker also had an anti-north thrust.

Founded by C.N. Annadurari, the DMK grew in strength and decided at its Tiruchi conference in 1956 to contest elections. Its manifesto for the elections in 1957 included a secessionist plank: "Each State should have full freedom to secede from the Indian Union if it so desires." In the manifesto for the next elections, adopted at Coimbatore in December 1961, the DMK said that it would work for the formation of a separate republic comprising Tamil Nadu, Kerala, Karnataka and Andhra Pradesh. Its capture of as many as 50 seats in the 206-seat Assembly in the 1962 elections created a stir within and outside Tamil Nadu.

In 1963 the Constitution was amended to stipulate that every candidate for election to parliament or to a State legislature should swear in the name of God, or should solemnly affirm, that he or she would uphold the sovereignty and integrity of India. Under the compulsion of this 16th Amendment the DMK altered its own party constitution on 3 November 1963 to drop the goal of an 'Independent Dravidanad'. A new clause was inserted in its place which said that the party would "strive for the formation of a closer Dravida Union of the four linguistic States of Tamil Nadu, Andhra Pradesh, Karnataka and Kerala, with as large powers as possible, within the framework of the sovereignty and integrity of India and of the Indian Constitution."

In the 1967 elections the DMK won an outright majority in the Tamil Nadu Assembly and displaced the Congress--which has been unable to recapture power since then. C.N. Annadurai became Chief Minister and, on his death in 1969, was succeeded by M. Karunanidhi as leader of the DMK. There was a split in 1972, when M.G. Ramachandran formed a rival Anna DMK (which later styled itself All India ADMK). It captured power in 1977. The Congress has had to ally itself with one or other of the two Dravidian parties in order to have a presence in the State assembly and to get some members elected to the Lok Sabha.

Andhra Pradesh, which adjoins Tamil Nadu, saw the emergence of a regional party much later, in 1983. But its success was spectacular. Telugu Desam was founded by N.T. Rama Rao as a party that would assert the self-respect of the people of Andhra Pradesh as against what was perceived as remote control of its government from New Delhi. The new party swept the 1983 Assembly polls, capturing as many as 202 of the 294 seats. An attempt by the Indira Gandhi government in 1984, through the State Governor, to topple N.T.Rama Rao boomeranged. Calling for fresh elections in 1985, he led his party to a repetition of the 1983 victory, again capturing 202 seats out of 294. It is a different matter that the electors of Andhra Pradesh disowned the TDP when they became dissatisfied with its rule. They switched their support back to the Congress (I) in the State Assembly polls that were held simultaneously with the Lok Sabha elections in November 1989.

The emergence of the Asom Gana Parishad was the outcome of widespread resentment at what was seen as the acquiescence of successive Congress (I) governments of Assam in the influx of migrants from Bangladesh. It was a case not only of Hindu refugees, as in the wake of the sub-continent's partition, but of immigrants both Hindu and Muslim. Poverty, even more acute in Bangladesh than in India on account of severe population pressure, has induced large numbers of Bangladesh Muslims to seek their livelihood in adjoining Indian States. Suspecting that the party in power at the Centre was letting the illegal immigrants stay in exchange for their votes in favour of the Congress (I), the students' organisation in Assam launched an agitation which made it impossible for the 1980 Lok Sabha elections to be held in 12 out of the 14 constituencies in the State. In the following year, the Centre had to abandon the attempt to conduct the 1981 Census in Assam. An accord was negotiated by the Rajiv Gandhi government in 1985 which sought to mollify Assamese sentiment not only on the issue of illegal immigrants but against what was perceived as neglect of the State's economic development. In the elections to the State Assembly held after the accord in 1985, the Asom Gana Parishad won an outright majority, with 65 seats out of the 126.

Two other large regional parties are the Shiromani Akali Dal in Punjab and the National Conference in Jammu & Kashmir. These regional parties, as well as the local units of the all-India parties, have not been able to stem the separatism and violence fomented by religious fanatics in recent years. This failure marred the conduct of the 1989 elections to the Lok Sabha. Secessionist militants in Kashmir Valley called for a boycott of the poll. Only one candidate--belonging to the National Conference--filed his nomination in the Srinagar constituency and was declared elected unopposed. The reason, it is widely believed, is not that this candidate was universally popular but that potential contestants felt intimidated. During the previous elections, except in 1980 when Dr. Farooq Abdullah (son of Sheikh Abdullah), was elected unopposed, there were four or more contestants in Srinagar constituency. The number of contestants was five in 1984, five in 1977, six in 1971 and four in 1967. In the November 1989 elections to the Lok Sabha, there was no constituency in the country other than Srinagar with only one candidate in the field.

In the other five Lok Sabha constituencies of Jammu & Kashmir, the combined strength of the electorate was 3,420,827. Out of these, only 1,023,562 cast valid votes. This marks a percentage of 29.9% as against the all-India voter turn-out of 59.94%. In J & K itself in earlier elections to the Lok Sabha, the voter turn-out ranged between 55% and 66%.

In Punjab which has 13 seats in the Lok Sabha, six were won by the Shiromani Akali Dal (Mann), three by Independents, two by the Congress (I) and one each by the Janata Dal and the Bahujan Samaj Party. The Akali candidates and successful Independents were closely identified with the militant section of the Akalis, and their success is attributed by many observers partly to intimidation by armed supporters of the candidates.

In addition to the bigger regional parties discussed above, there are a large number specific to an area or to ethnic groups. Those recognised by the Election Commission and having at least one representative in either House of Parliament include: the All India Forward Bloc; Revolutionary Socialist Party; Sikkim Sangram Parishad; Kerala Congress (J); Bahujan Samaj Party; Muslim League; Shiv Sena; Maharashtrawadi Gomantak Party; Kerala Congress (M); and Jharkhand Mukti Morcha.

(iii) Stars in Political Wars

It is remarkable that the founders and present leaders of all the three southern regional parties have been personalities prominent in the film world. C.N. Annadurai, founder of the DMK, was a popular script writer. He became Chief Minister of Tamil Nadu long before actor Ronald Reagan was elected as President of the U.S.A. Annadurai was succeeded on his death by M. Karunanidhi, another script writer.

M.G. Ramachandran, a screen idol, founded the AIADMK--which is a regional party though it carries the prefix 'All India'--as a rival to the DMK. On the death of MGR in December 1988 there was a tussle for the succession between two film actresses--his widow Janaki and Jayalalitha, a younger actress who had starred opposite MGR in many a film. Jayalalitha emerged as the winner. Sivaji Ganesan is among other prominent film personalities who have been active in Tamil Nadu politics.

N.T. Rama Rao who founded the TDP is the Andhra counterpart of MGR in terms of popularity with film viewers. In the elections to the Andhra Pradesh Assembly that were held in November 1989 along with the Lok Sabha poll, the prominent candidates included the actor Krishna, from the Eluru constituency, and the actress Jamuna from Rajahmundry. Both won the seats for the Congress (I).

The first major incursion of a film personality into politics in north India was in December 1984. Prime Minister Rajiv Gandhi persuaded his close friend Amitabh Bachchan, the matinee idol, to become the Congress (I) candidate for election to the Lok Sabha from the Allahabad constituency in Uttar Pradesh. Pitted against him was H.N. Bahuguna, a veteran politician who had served for several years as Chief Minister of Uttar Pradesh. The film star trounced the politician.

Other film personalities utilised in recent years for election campaigning in some parts of north India include R.K. Govil, who played Rama in the immensely popular TV serialisation of the Ramayana epic. Congress (I)'s Govil was countered by the opposition with another film actor, Raj Babbar. During the November 1989 elections, a prominent campaigner for the National Front was the popular film star Shatrughan Sinha.

(iv) 1989: Tense Run-up

The strengthening of the Janata Dal by its alliance with three major regional parties in a National Front was followed by a move that was to prove an even more potent factor in the outcome of the 1989 elections to the Lok Sabha. This was the forging of seat adjustments by the National Front with the BJP, on the one hand, and with the two Communist parties on the other. It was intended to ensure, as far as possible, a virtual one-to-one contest against the Congress (I). Despite hard bargaining, the effort succeeded by and large.

Dislodging the Congress (I) from power at the Centre was the only objective that these parties had in common. There was no shared policy or programme. On the contrary, spokesmen of the two Communist parties constantly denounced the BJP as a 'Hindu communal' organisation. Some of the leaders of the Janata Dal expressed the same disparaging view of the BJP.

Against this background, the escalation of controversy on Ramjanmabhoomi vs. Babri Masjid at Ayodhya in Uttar Pradesh threatened to break up the anti-Congress front. The Viswa Hindu Parishad had announced its intention of conducting the 'Shilanyas' (foundation laying) for a new and large temple at Ayodhya. This was to be on the site where, according to them, the forces of Babur who invaded India and established the Mughal empire demolished in 1528 an old temple commemorating the place of birth of Lord Rama and built a mosque on its ruins. Whereas the BJP supported the VHP's plan, it was opposed by the Babri Masjid Action Committee comprising representatives of a number of Muslim organisations. They held that there had been no temple at the site, and said they would resist any attempt to demolish the mosque named after Babur. Tensions mounted as the polling dates approached.

V.P. Singh publicly distanced himself from the BJP by refusing to share any platform with it during his election campaign tour of

Uttar Pradesh. He had earlier called more than once on the Shahi Imam of Delhi's Jama Masjid--as did H.K.L. Bhagat on behalf of Congress president Rajiv Gandhi--to seek the support of the Imam, and through him of the Muslim community, in the forthcoming elections. From the side of the Congress (I) which has traditionally befriended the Muslim minority and enjoyed its electoral support, except during the 1977 elections in the wake of the internal emergency, Rajiv Gandhi declared at Ayodhya during his election campaign in Uttar Pradesh that his party, if returned to power, would bring about Ram Rajya. This is a hallowed expression which denotes the reign of justice as during the rule of Lord Rama of the Indian epic, regarded by Hindus as a human incarnation of God.

There was relief all round when, despite the invoking of religious sentiment on both sides, the Shilanyas at Ayodhya passed off without incident . But the likely effect of the whole controversy on the Lok Sabha elections became a subject of lively speculation among political pundits. Some thought that the peaceful laying of the temple's foundation would swing many Hindu votes in favour of the Congress (I) since it had been facilitated by a State government run by the Congres (I). Others, however, were of the view that the prolonged non-committal attitude of the Congress (I) on the basic issue of Ramjanmabhoomi had already alienated Hindu sentiment. As for the effect of the Shilanyas on Muslim voters, it was widely expected to be negative.

(v) New Political Configuration

In any case, Ayodhya was but one issue in the elections. Allegations of corruption in governmental purchases of large value, including and in particular of defence equipment from abroad, figured much longer and much more prominently in the election campaign by non-Congress parties. The actual outcome of the elections was determined primarily by the working unity and seat adjustment among the non-Congress parties. As in early 1977, a broad alliance of non-Congress parties brought about a change, towards the close of 1989, in the political complexion of the government at the Centre. Because of the high degree of opposition unity, the Congress (I) obtained in 1989, as it had in 1977, a lower percentage of seats in the Lok Sabha than its percentage share of the total vote. In every other election to the Lok Sabha the case was the opposite. Table VI shows the number and percentage of seats won, and the percentage of votes polled, by various political parties in the November 1989 elections to the Lok Sabha.

TABLE VI

Party Position in Ninth Lok Sabha

Party	*Seats Won*	*% of total seats **	*% of votes polled*	*No. of candidates***	*Success ratio*
Cong. (I)	194	37.02	39.33	505	38.41
Janata Dal	142	27.1	17.73	245	57.95
BJP	86	16.4	11.56	226	38.05
CPM	32	6.1	6.32	63	50.79
CPI	11	2.1	2.61	51	21.56
AIADMK	11	2.1	1.51	11	100.00
Telugu Desam	2	.38	3.32	34	5.9
IC (S)	1	.19	0.33	14	7.2
Others	33	6.38	11.68	1424	2.3
Ind.	12	2.9	5.61	3518	.34

*The total number of seats for which elections were held was 524.

**The total number of candidates was 6091.

Table VII indicates the performance of the main political parties State-wise.

TABLE VII

Party performance--State-wise

No. of seats	State/U.T.	Cong (I)	Janata Dal	BJP	CPM	CPI	Other Parties	Independents
	*State**							
42	Andhra Pradesh	39	0	0	0	0	3	0
2	Arunachal Pradesh	2	0	0	0	0	0	0
54	Bihar	4	31	9	1	4	5	0
1	Goa	0	0	0	0	0	1	0
26	Gujarat	3	11	12	0	0	0	0
9	Harayana	3	6	0	0	0	0	0
4	Himachal Pradesh	1	0	3	0	0	0	0
6	Jammu & Kashmir	2	0	0	0	0	3	1
28	Karnataka	27	1	0	0	0	0	0
20	Kerala	14	0	0	2	0	4	0
39	Madhya Pradesh	8	3	27	0	0	0	1
48	Maharashtra	28	5	10	0	1	1	3
2	Manipur	2	0	0	0	0	0	0
2	Meghalaya	2	0	0	0	0	0	0
1	Mizoram	1	0	0	0	0	0	0
1	Nagaland	1	0	0	0	0	0	0
21	Orissa	3	17	0	1	0	0	0
13	Punjab	2	1	0	0	0	7	3
25	Rajasthan	0	11	13	1	0	0	0
1	Sikkim	0	0	0	0	0	1	0
38	Tamil Nadu	26	0	0	0	1	11	0

No. of seats	State/U.T.	Cong (I)	Janata Dal	BJP	CPM	CPI	Other Parties	Independents
2	Tripura	2	0	0	0	0	0	0
85	Uttar Pradesh	15	54	8	1	2	3	2
41	West Bengal	4	0	0	26	3	8	0
* (Among the 25 States, Assam did not go to the polls.)								
	U.T.							
1	Andaman & Nicobar	1	0	0	0	0	0	0
1	Chandigarh	0	1	0	0	0	0	0
1	Dadra & Nagar Haveli	0	0	0	0	0	0	1
7	Delhi	2	1	4	0	0	0	0
1	Lakshadweep	1	0	0	0	0	0	0
1	Pondicherry	1	0	0	0	0	0	0
1	Daman & Diu	0	0	0	0	0	0	0
524		194	142	86	32	11	47	12

Before considering the performance of the main political parties in the November 1989 election to the Lok Sabha, it may be noticed that the total number of Independent candidates who got elected is only 12 out of 524. On the other hand, the number of Independent candidates was even higher than in previous elections, with the consequence that the average number of contestants per constituency rose to 12 from 10 in 1984 (see Figure 4).

One reason for the proliferation of non-serious candidates is the very small deposit that is required to be made by a candidate, and which he or she loses in the event of failing to secure at least one-sixth of the votes cast. The sum was fixed at Rs. 500 in the case of candidature for the Lok Sabha, and Rs.250 for State Assembly elections, in connection with the elections of 1951-52. These sums have remained unchanged despite the steep fall in the value of the

LOK SABHA ELECTIONS PTI

Average Number of Candidates per Constituency

Year	1952	1957	1962	1967	1971	1977	1980	1984	1989
Avg. no. of Cand. per Constituency	**4**	**3**	**4**	**5**	**5**	**5**	**9**	**10**	**12**

Fig. 4

rupee over the last four decades. Independent candidates accounted for as many as 3,746 of the total of 4,263 candidates who forfeited their deposits in the elections to the eighth Lok Sabha held in 1984. While it costs the non-serious candidate--or those sponsoring him for their own reasons--little, the administration has to incur substantial expenditure on printing ballot papers of increasing length--apart from the bewilderment and inconvenience caused to voters and to polling officials. Measures for discouraging frivolous candidates are among the proposals made to the Government by the Election Commission for electoral reform. Curiously however, the major political parties have not given an important place in their schemes of electoral reform (see section iv of Chapter 4) to the need to discourage the filing of nomination by non-serious candidates.

The strength of the Congress slumped from 415 in the eighth Lok Sabha to 194 even though its share of the popular vote declined by only 8.77 percentage points. Figure 5 depicts the performance of the Congress in the successive Lok Sabha elections.

Among the non-Congress parties, the Janata Dal secured the highest tally of 142 seats. This is in contrast to the position in the eighth Lok Sabha, in which the highest number of seats held by a non-Congress party (Telugu Desam) was 28. It was the first time that a State party was the largest single opposition group in the Lok Sabha.

While the Janata Dal did well in the 1989 elections, its partners in the National Front did not. As against the Dal's 142 seats the Telugu Desam Party could win only two seats and the Indian Congress (Secular) one seat. The DMK drew a blank in Tamil Nadu, while the Asom Gana Parishad could contribute no seats since Assam did not go to the polls. In the result, the National Front had a tally of only 145 seats.

LOK SABHA ELECTIONS PTI

Congress in Lok Sabha Elections

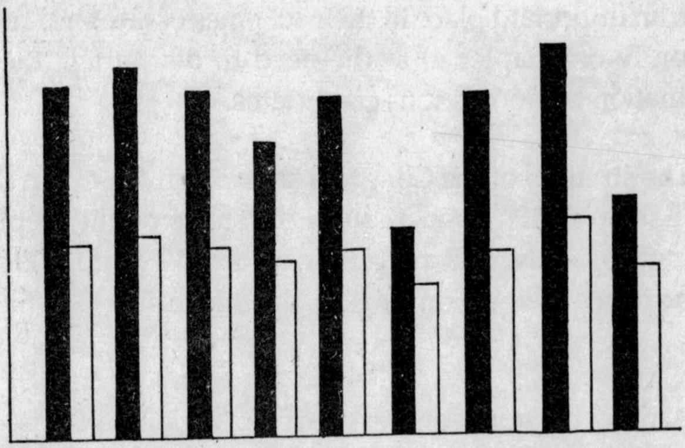

Year	1952	1957	1962	1967	1971	1977	1980	1984	1989
■ Seats	364	371	361	283	352	154	353	415	194
□ Votes%	45.0	47.8	44.7	40.8	43.7	34.3	42.7	48 1	39.33

Fig. 5

BJP emerged second among the non-Congress parties, after the Janata Dal. It registered a spectacular increase in its presence, from a mere two seats in the eighth Lok Sabha to 86. Figure 6 depicts the performance of the BJP in the successive Lok Sabha elections.

The steady progress of the Bharatiya Jan Sangh from its modest beginning in the first elections to the Lok Sabha in 1952, till 1967, has been noticed earlier, in Chapter 3 (i). Table VIII shows the subsequent performance of the Jan Sangh in terms of the percentage of the total vote won by it as well as the States in which it accounted for more than 10% of the vote. (The BJS merged in the Janata Party in 1979 and re-emerged as the BJP after the 1980 elections.)

TABLE VIII

Areas of BJP's Influence

Year	*No. of Lok Sabha seats won*	*% of all-India vote*	*% of vote State-wise*
1971	22	7.4	Bihar (12.1)
			Haryana (11.2)
			Himachal Pradesh (10.6)
			Jammu & Kashmir (12.2)
			Madhya Pradesh (33.6)
			Rajasthan (12.4)
			Uttar Pradesh (12.3)
			Chandigarh (23.3)
			Delhi (29.6)
1984	2	7.4	Gujarat (18.6)
			Himachal Pradesh (23.3)
			Madhya Pradesh (30.0)

LOK SABHA ELECTIONS PTI

BJP in Lok Sabha Elections

Bharatiya Jan Sangh from 1952 to 1971.
In 1977 & 1980, BJP did not exist as a separate party.

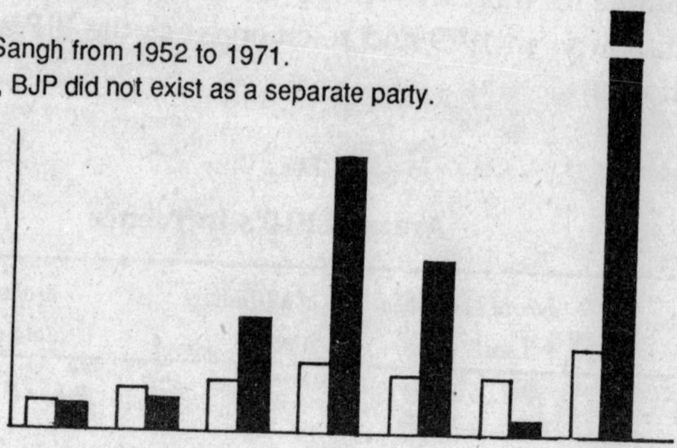

Year	1952	1957	1962	1967	1971	1984	1989
Seats	3	4	14	35	22	2	86
Votes %	3.1	5.9	6.4	9.4	7.4	7.4	11.3

Fig. 6

Year	*No. of Lok Sabha seats won*	*% of all-India vote*	*% of vote State-wise*
			Maharashtra (10.1)
			Rajasthan (23.7)
			Delhi (18.8)
1989	86	11.56	Bihar (12.98)
			Gujarat (30.46)
			Himachal Pradesh (45.25)
			Madhya Pradesh (40.51)
			Maharashtra (23.72)
			Rajasthan (29.63)
			Delhi (26.19)

The CPI (M) ranks third among the non-Congress parties in the ninth Lok Sabha, with 32 seats. This marks a significant increase from the 21 seats it had in the eighth Lok Sabha. Figure 7 depicts the performance of the CPM in successive elections to the Lok Sabha.

CPI's strength rose to 11 seats in the ninth Lok Sabha as against six in the previous House. Figure 8 shows the performance of the CPI in the successive Lok Sabha elections.

(vi) Northern 'Waves' and the South

There has been a pattern of contrast between north and south since the 1977 elections to the Lok Sabha. That year an anti-Congress wave swept the north--though the extent of the swing away from the party was exaggerated, in terms of seats, by our electoral system of first-past-the-post. In contrast, the south where the internal emergency bore less hard on citizens, voted for the Congress by and large. In 1980 there was a swing back to the Congress in the north, while there was little difference in the party's tally south of the Vindhyas. Following the assassination of Prime Minister Indira Gandhi, a wave of sympathy for her sole

LOK SABHA ELECTIONS PTI

CPM in Lok Sabha Elections

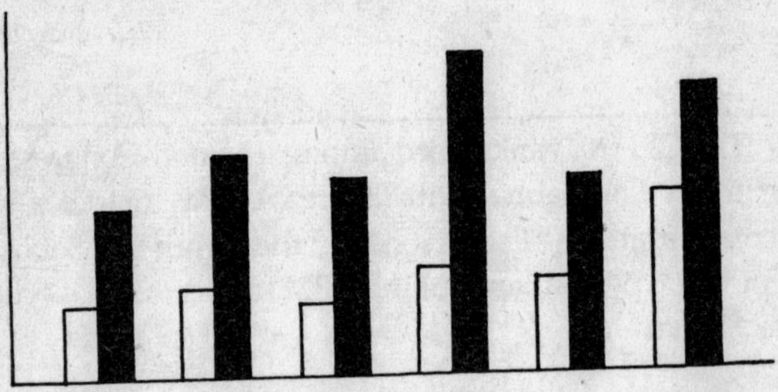

Year	1967	1971	1977	1980	1984	1989
Seats	19	25	22	36	22	32
Votes %	4.4	5.1	4.3	6.1	5.7	10.01

Fig. 7

LOK SABHA ELECTIONS **PTI**

CPI in Lok Sabha Elections

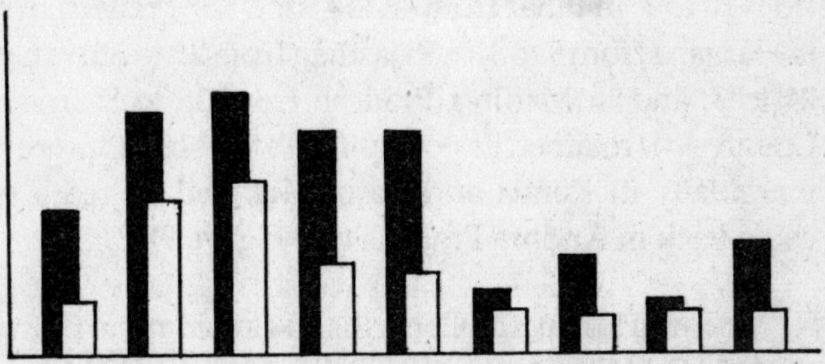

Year	1952	1957	1962	1967	1971	1977	1980	1984	1989
■ Seats	16	27	29	23	23	7	11	6	12
□ Votes%	3.3	8.9	9.9	5.0	4.7	2.8	2.6	2.7	2.2

Fig. 8

surviving son, Rajiv Gandhi, enabled him to lead the Congress (I) to mighty victories in most of the northern States in the December 1984 elections to the eighth Lok Sabha. But the sympathy wave did not wash away the Telugu Desam Party in Andhra Pradesh.

That all-India parties other than the Congress have failed, over the four decades since independence, to spread their roots in the south as a whole became evident in the latest elections to the Lok Sabha in 1989, as earlier in 1977.

Across the entire northern belt there was a dramatic fall in the number of Congress candidates elected to the Lok Sabha: in Orissa from 20 to 3; in Bihar from 48 to 4; in Uttar Pradesh from 82 to 15; in Haryana from 9 to 3; in Rajasthan from 25 to nil; in Gujarat from 24 to 3; and in Madhya Pradesh from 38 to 8. In contrast, the Congress (I) retained its position in Tamil Nadu, improved its tally marginally in Kerala and Karnataka; and staged a spectacular come-back in Andhra Pradesh (see Figure 9).

In Tamil Nadu, the Congress (I) gained more from its alliance with the AIADMK than its southern partner led by the popular film actress Jayalalitha. A PTI computer-aided analysis showed that whereas in the Assembly elections of early 1989 the Congress (I) contesting alone, polled only 20% of the votes, in the Lok Sabha elections of November, thanks to the alliance, it secured 37% of the votes and won 24 seats.

On the other hand, the two factions of the AIADMK secured nearly 30% of the votes in the Assembly polls but now, by conceding a larger share of Lok Sabha seats to the Congress (I), the AIADMK unified under Jayalalitha's leadership contested only 11 seats which it won on 17.53% of the popular vote. The party gave a large share of seats to the Congress (I) apprently anticipating that in a future Assembly poll adjustment it could claim, in return, a high share of seats.

The DMK secured 25.20% of the popular vote in the Lok Sabha elections although it drew a total blank in terms of seats. It

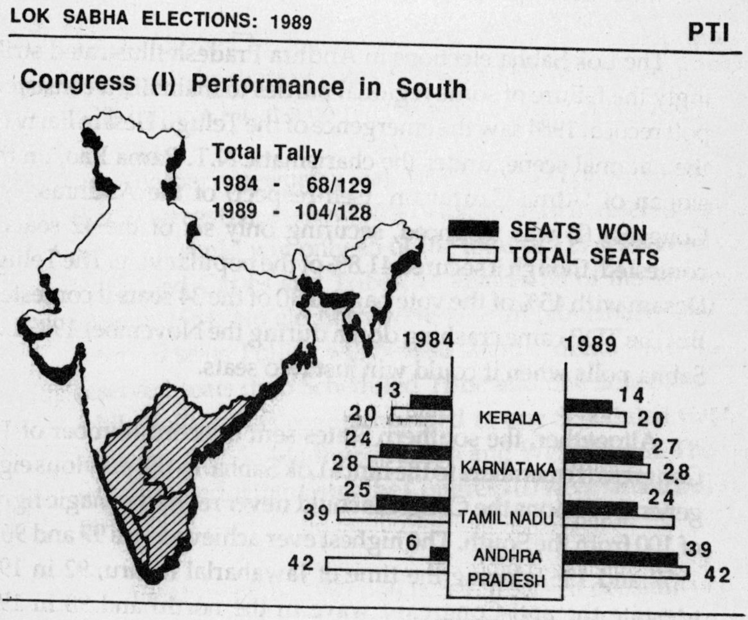
LOK SABHA ELECTIONS: 1989
PTI
Congress (I) Performance in South
Total Tally
1984 - 68/129
1989 - 104/128
SEATS WON
TOTAL SEATS
1984
1989
13
20
KERALA
14
20
24
28
KARNATAKA
27
28
25
39
TAMIL NADU
24
6
42
ANDHRA PRADESH
39
42

Fig. 9

In India's four metropolitan cities, voters shifted their choice from the Congress (I), mainly in favour of the BJP and CPI (M).

A PTI computer analysis showed that in Delhi, Bombay, Calcutta and Madras, with 20 seats and 19.8 million voters, the Congress (I) lost ten seats from its 1984 tally of 17.

The BJP-Shiv Sena alliance captured eight seats and the CPM two, while one seat each was won by the Janata Dal and the United Communist Party of India (UCPI).

The Shiv Sena, a regional party having its base among Maharashtrian Hindus, made a good showing in the highly cosmopolitan and commercialised western metropolis. However, voters in high-income areas--whether in South Bombay, Madras South or Calcutta North-West--continued to show their preference for the Congress (I). In Bombay South, Murali Deora, president of the Bombay regional Congress (I) committee, retained his seat but by a reduced margin of 17,789 votes as compared to the 1984 margin of 1,05,278.

In Delhi, the main power tussle continued, as in earlier years, to be between the Congress (I) and the BJP which controlled both the Delhi Corporation and the Metropolitan Council in the 'seventies. The BJP captured all the seven Lok Sabha seats in the post-emergency elections of 1977. In the 1984 elections, held very soon after Indira Gandhi's assassination, the Congress (I) regained all the Lok Sabha seats. But in 1989 the BJP again managed to wrest four seats from the Congress (I) while one seat was won by the Janata Dal under the seat adjustment between partners in the alliance against the Congress (I).

(viii) A 'Hung' Lok Sabha

The cumulative outcome of the November 1989 elections was a 'hung' Lok Sabha, with no single party commanding a majority on its own. It was a situation comparable, to a limited extent, to the situation which arose twenty years earlier when, following the split in the ruling party in 1969, the bigger Congress faction led by Prime Minister Indira Gandhi did not command a majority in the fourth Lok Sabha. The government was able to continue with the support of the Communist and Left parties. Whereas the 'hung' period of the fourth Lok Sabha, elected in 1967, was relatively brief, the ninth Lok Sabha was 'hung' from the start.

The Congress with 194 seats was the largest single party. But it was not possible for the party to head a coalition, or to form a minority government with support from outside, since the political parties committed to keeping the Congress (I) out of power commanded a total membership of 274, constituting more than half the strength of the Lok Sabha.

Nor could a coalition government be formed by the anti-Congress (I) parties which had entered into seat adjustment, because of their ideological differences. The National Front, in effect meaning the Janata Dal, therefore formed a government with support, from outside, of the BJP and the two Communist parties. The piquancy of the situation was illustrated by the exchange of letters between the National Front and the BJP prior to the formation of the new government. N.T. Rama Rao, as chairman of the National Front, and Vishwanath Pratap Singh as convener, wrote to L.K. Advani, president of the BJP, on 28 November 1989:

"We are sure that you agree with us that the people of India have given a clear and unmistakable verdict against the Congress (I) misrule and for a change of government at the Centre. The seat adjustments among the various opposition parties have greatly helped us in defeating the Congress (I). It is now the sacred duty of all of us to see that this mandate of the people is not frustrated and the formation of a non-Congress (I) government to give effect to the hopes and aspirations of the people is not delayed.

1969, Congress (I) Prime Ministers have also been the supreme authority with the party, whether or not holding formal office as Congress president. The second and more important reason, which in part accounts for the first, is the charisma of Indira Gandhi which made her the principal and indispensable vote-getter within the party during the 16 years of her prime ministership as well as the three years out of office during 1977-79. Rajiv Gandhi initially appeared to have inherited the charisma, but this impression has weakened. There is no guarantee that a Central government that may be formed by the Congress in future will be free of factional tensions.

(x) Shifting Scene in the States

Table X presents a comprehensive picture of the changes in the political complexion of State Assemblies following successive elections. It records the performance, in terms of seats and votes, of the two top contenders, whether all-India or regional parties, in the Assembly elections held in each of the 25 States and in Pondicherry which is the only one out of the Union Territories to have a legislature. Some more parties are noticed in the case of States where they have played an important role, in coalition governments or otherwise. Information is given from the time of the first elections in a Union Territory or State (in its present territorial shape in the case of States that were reorganised).

It will be seen that in many State Assemblies there has been a marked disproportion--as in the case of the successive Lok Sabhas --between a party's share of votes and of seats.

Secondly, there was in the initial years a preponderance of Independents among those elected to the Assemblies of the States in the north-east, specially Manipur, Mizoram and Nagaland. Over the years, however, voters in the north-east too have begun to choose between candidates of different political parties, regional or all India.

Most of the States went through their most recent elections either in November 1989 or in February 1990. In Andhra Pradesh, Goa, Karnataka, Sikkim and Uttar Pradesh, Assembly elections were held along with the November 1989 Lok Sabha poll. Out of the three major States, the anti-Congress alliance fared badly in two. Telugu Desam suffered the same severe set-back in the Andhra Pradesh Assembly election as in the Lok Sabha poll. Karnataka voters, too switched back their support to the Congress (I) in what seemed like an expression of disapproval of the factionalism which had brought down the previous government run by the Janata Party. However, in Uttar Pradesh, which has a population larger than the combined population of the other four States that had Assembly elections in November 1989, the party alliance led by the Janata Dal dislodged the Congress from power.

TABLE IX

Turn-over of Congress (I) Chief Ministers

Name of Chief Minister	*From*	*To*
	ANDHRA PRADESH	
M. Chenna Reddy	March 1978	October 1980
T.Anjaiah	October 1980	February 1982
B. Venkatarama Reddy	February 1982	September 1982
K.V. Bhaskara Reddy	September 1982	January 1983
	MAHARASHTRA	
S.B. Chavan	February 1975	April 1977
Vasant Dada Patil	April 1977	July 1978
A.R. Antulay	June 1980	January 1982
Baba Saheb Bhosale	January 1982	February 1983
Vasant Dada Patil	February 1983	June 1985

S.P. Nilangekar	June 1985	March 1986
S.B. Chavan	March 1986	June 1988
	UTTAR PRADESH	
T.N. Singh	October 1970	April 1971
Kamalapati Tripathi	April 1971	November 1973
H.N. Bahuguna	November 1973	January 1976
N.D. Tiwari	January 1976	June 1977
V.P. Singh	June 1980	June 1982
Shripati Mishra	June 1982	August 1984
N.D.Tiwari	August 1984	September 1985
Vir Bahadur Singh	September 1985	June 1988
N.D. Tiwari	June 1988	November 1989

TABLE X

Principal Parties in State Assemblies

Year	*Total seats*	*Party*	*Seats won*	*% of votes*
1955-57	(i)	ANDHRA PRADESH		
(Elections were held in the Andhra region in 1955 and in Telengana in 1957)	301	Congress	187	41.7
		People's Democratic Front	22	7.6
		Krishikar Lok Party	22	5.1
1962	300	Congress	177	47.3
		CPI	51	19.5
1967	287	Congress	165	45.4
		Swantantra	29	9.8

Year	Total seats	Party	Seats won	% of votes
1972	287	Congress (I)	219	52.3
		CPI	7	6.0
1978	294	Congress (I)	175	39.3
		Janata Party	60	28.9
1983	294	Telugu Desam	202	46.3
		Congress (I)	60	33.6
1985	294	Telugu Desam	202	46.2
		Congress (I)	50	37.5
1989	294	Congress (I)	180	N.A.
		TDP	74	N.A.
		(ii) ARUNACHAL PRADESH		
1978	30	Janata Party	17	42.1
		People's Party of Arunachal	8	30.2
1980	30	Congress (I)	13	42.6
		People's Party of Arunachal	13	41.0
1984	30	Congress (I)	21	43.07
		People's Party of Aruncahal	4	14.27
1990	60	Congress (I)	37	N.A.
		Janata Dal	11	N.A.
		(iii) ASSAM		
1952	105	Congress	75	43.5
		Socialist Party	4	13.3
1957	108	Congress	71	52.4
		Praja Socialist Party	8	12.7
1962	105	Congress	79	48.3

Year	Total seats	Party	Seats won	% of votes
		All Party Hill Leaders Conference	11	5.5
1967	125	Congress	73	43.6
		APHLC	9	3.5
1972	114	Congress (I)	95	53.2
		Socialist Party	4	5.8
1978	126	Janata Party	53	27.6
		Indian Congress (Socialist)	26	23.6
1983	109	Congress (I)	91	52.5
		Plains Tribal Council of Assam	3	4.7
1985	126	Asom Gana Parishad	65	35.0
		Congress (I)	25	23.2
		(iv) BIHAR		
1952	330	Congress	240	41.4
		Jharkand Party	33	N.A.
		Socialist Party	23	18.2
1957	318	Congress	210	41.9
		Praja Socialist Party	31	16.20
1962	318	Congress	185	41.35
		Swatantra	50	17.25
1967	318	Congress	128	30.08
		SSP	68	17.62
1969	318	Congress	118	33.08
		SSP	68	13.46
1972	318	Congress (I)	168	33.12
		CPI	35	6.94
1977	324	Janata Party	214	46.68
		Congress (I)	57	23.58

Year	Total seats	Party	Seats won	% of votes
1980	324	Congress (I)	169	34.20
		Janata Party (Secular)	42	15.5
1985	324	Congress (I)	196	39.30
		Lok Dal	46	14.72
1990	323	Janata Dal	121	N.A.
		(316 results Congress (I) declared)	71	N.A.

(V) GOA, DAMAN AND DIU

(They constituted a Union Territory till 1987, when Goa became a State while Daman and Diu remained a Union Territory.)

Year	Total seats	Party	Seats won	% of votes
1967	30	Maharashtrawadi Gomantak	16	40.4
		United Goans (Sequeira Group)	12	38.0
1972	30	MAG	18	38.3
		UGS	10	32.5
1977	30	MAG	15	38.5
		Congress (I)	10	28.9
1980	30	Congress (Urs)	20	38.4
		MAG	7	36.4
1984	30	Congres (I)	18	39.5
		MAG	8	21.1
1989	40	Congress (I)	20	N.A.
(Goa)		MAG	18	N.A.

(vi) GUJARAT

Year	Total seats	Party	Seats won	% of votes
1962	154	Congress	113	50.84
		Swatantra	26	24.43
1967	168	Congress	93	45.74
		Swatantra	66	38.19
1972	168	Congress (I)	140	50.93

Year	Total seats	Party	Seats won	% of votes
		Congress (O)	16	23.49
1975	182	Congress (I)	75	40.7
		Congress (O)	56	23.6
1980	182	Congress (I)	141	51.04
		Janata Party	21	22.77
1985	182	Congress (I)	149	55.55
		Janata Party	14	19.25
1990	182	Janata Dal	70	29.68
		BJP	67	26.50

(vii) HARYANA

Year	Total seats	Party	Seats won	% of votes
1967	81	Congress	48	41.3
		Bharatiya Jan Sangh	12	14.4
1968	81	Congress	48	43.8
		Vishal Haryana Parishad	16	14.9
1972	81	Congress (I)	52	46.9
		Congress (O)	12	10.8
1977	90	Janata Party	75	46.7
		VHP	5	6.0
1982	90 -	Congress (I)	36	37.6
		Lok Dal	31	23.9
1987	90	Lok Dal	60	38.58
		BJP	16	10.08

(viii) HIMACHAL PRADESH

Year	Total seats	Party	Seats won	% of votes
1967	60	Congress (I)	34	42.19
		Bharatiya Jan Sangh	7	13.87
1972	68	Congress (I)	53	53.24

ASSEMBLY ELECTIONS : 1990 **PTI**

Party Position in Gujarat Assembly

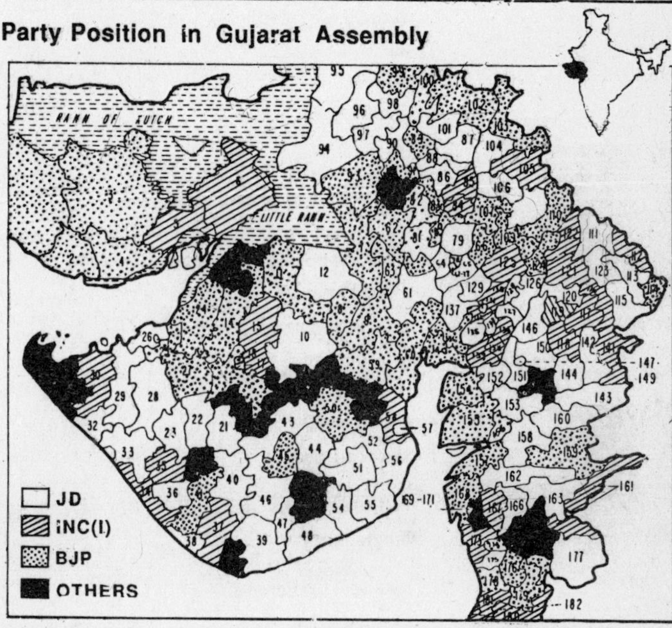

Fig. 10

Year	Total seats	Party	Seats won	% of votes
		BJS	5	7.75
1977	68	Janata Party	53	49.01
		Congress (I)	9	27.74
1982	68	Congress (I)	31	42.52
		BJP	29	35.16
1985	68	Congress (I)	58	55.46
		BJP	7	30.6
1990	68	BJP	44	N.A.
		Janata Dal	11	N.A.

(ix) JAMMU & KASHMIR

Year	Total seats	Party	Seats won	% of votes
1962	75	J & K National Conference	70	67.0
		Praja Parishad	3	17.5
1967	75	Congress	61	53.0
		National Conference	8	17.1
1972	75	Congress (I)	58	55.4
		Jamat-i-Islami	5	7.2
1977	76	National Conference	47	46.2
		Janata Party	13	23.7
1983	75	National Conference	46	47.3
		Congress (I)	26	30.3
1987	76	National Conference	40	32.99
		Congress (I)	26	20.2

(x) KARNATAKA

Year	Total seats	Party	Seats won	% of votes
1957	208	Congress	149	51.9
		Praja Socialist Party	18	14.1
1962	208	Congress	138	50.2
		PSP	20	14.1

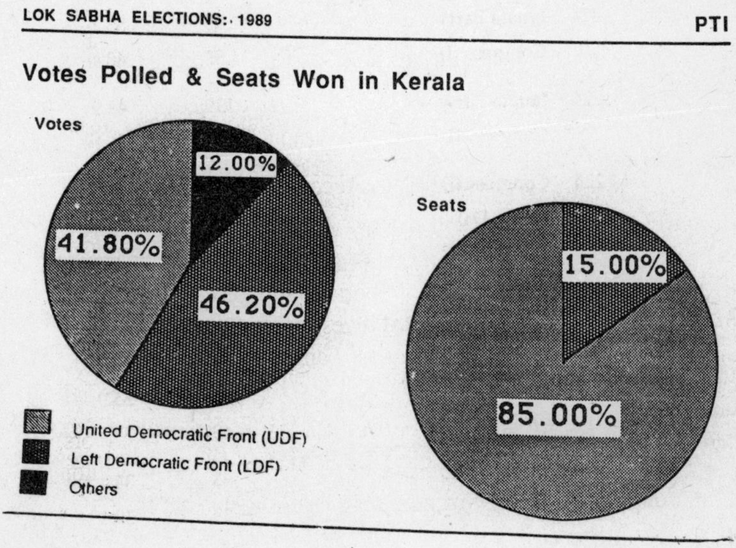
LOK SABHA ELECTIONS: 1989
PTI
Votes Polled & Seats Won in Kerala
Votes
12.00%
41.80%
46.20%
Seats
15.00%
85.00%
United Democratic Front (UDF)
Left Democratic Front (LDF)
Others

Fig. 11

Year	Total seats	Party	Seats won	% of votes
1967	216	Congress	126	48.4
		PSP	20	8.9
1972	216	Congress (I)	165	52.2
		Congress (O)	24	26.2
1978	224	Congress (I)	149	44.2
		Janata Party	59	37.9
1983	224	Janata Party	95	33.1
		Congress (I)	82	40.4
1985	224	Janata Party	139	43.9
		Congress (I)	66	41.1
1989	224	Congress (I)	177	N.A.
		Janata Dal	24	N.A.

(xi) KERALA

Year	Total seats	Party	Seats won	% of votes
1957	126	CPI	60	35.0
		Congress	43	38.1
1960	126	Congress	63	34.4
		CPI	29	39.1
1965	133	CPM	40	19.9
		Congress	36	33.3
1967	133	CPM	52	23.5
		CPI	19	8.6
		Samyukta Socialist Party	19	8.4
1970	133	Congress (I)	30	17.6
		CPM	29	23.8
1977	140	Congress (I)	38	20.0
		CPI	23	9.9
1980	140	CPM	35	19.4

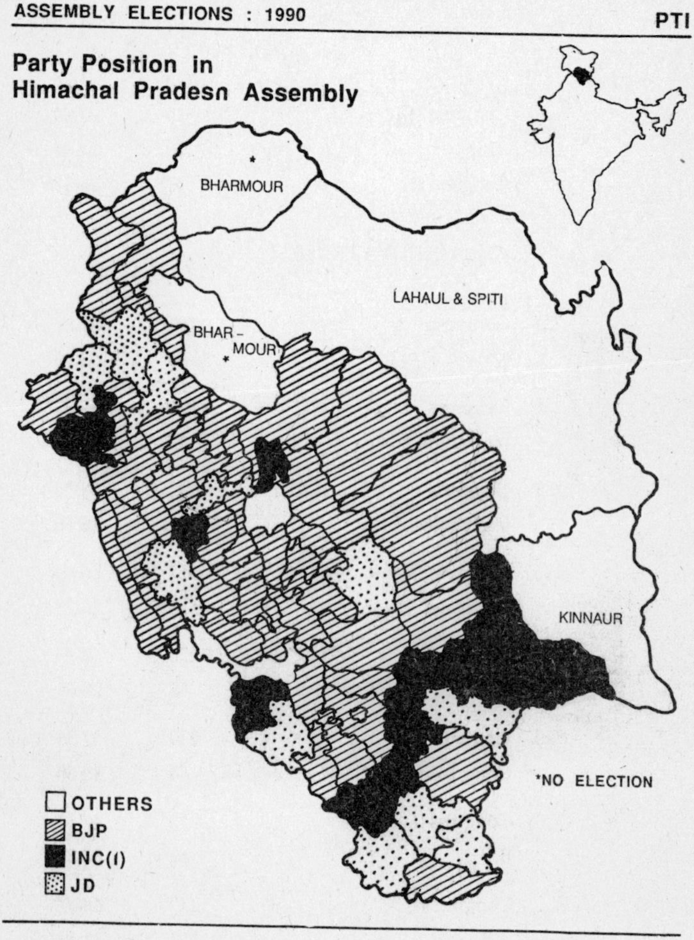
ASSEMBLY ELECTIONS : 1990
PTI
Party Position in
Himachal Pradesn Assembly
BHARMOUR
LAHAUL & SPITI
BHAR-
MOUR
KINNAUR
*NO ELECTION
OTHERS
BJP
INC(I)
JD

Fig. 12

Year	Total seats	Party	Seats won	% of votes
		Congress (Urs)--Indian Congress Socialist	21	11.0
1982	140	CPM	26	18.8
		Congress (I)	20	11.9
1987	140	CPM	38	22.84
		Congress (I)	33	24.81

(xii) MADHYA PRADESH

Year	Total seats	Party	Seats won	% of votes
1952	232	Congress	191	46.80
		KMPP	8	3.90
1957	288	Congress	232	49.83
		Jan Sangh	10	9.98
1962	288	Congress	142	38.54
		Jan Sangh	41	16.66
1967	296	Congress	167	40.69
		Jan Sangh	78	28.28
1972	295	Congress	220	47.93
		Jan Sangh	48	28.68
1977	320	Janata Party	230	47.36
		Congress (I)	84	35.80
1980	320	Congress (I)	246	47.52
		BJP	60	30.33
1985	320	Congress (I)	250	48.87
		BJP	58	32.42
1990	320	BJP	214	37.15
		Congress (I)	61	31.88

(xiii) MAHARASHTRA

Year	Total seats	Party	Seats won	% of votes
1962	264	Congress	215	52.89
		Peasants & Workers Party	15	7.5

ASSEMBLY ELECTIONS : 1990 **PTI**

Party Position in Madhya Pradesh Assembly

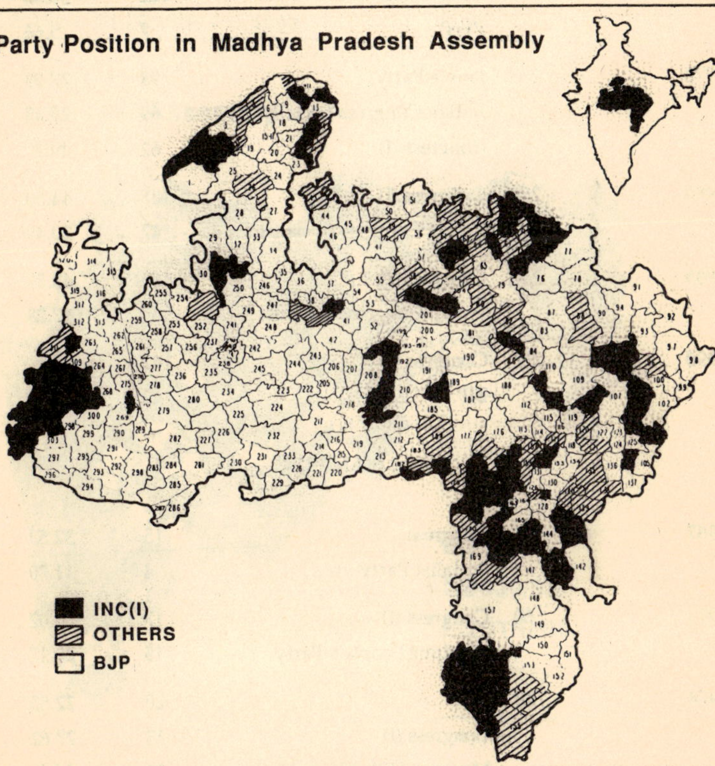

Fig. 13

Year	*Total seats*	*Party*	*Seats won*	*% of votes*
1990	60	Congress (I)	24	44.2
		Janata Dal	10	28.58

(xv) MEGHALAYA

Year	*Total seats*	*Party*	*Seats won*	*% of votes*
1972	60	All Party Hill Leaders Conference	32	35.7
		Congress (I)	9	12.0
1978	60	Congress (I)	20	29.0
		APHLC	16	24.9
1983	60	Congress (I)	25	27.7
		APHLC	15	25.1
		Hill State People's Democratic Party	15	19.3
1988	59	Congress (I)	22	32.65
		Hill People's Union	19	26.84

(xvi) MIZORAM

Year	*Total seats*	*Party*	*Seats won*	*% of votes*
1972	30	Independents	24	67.6
		Congress (I)	6	30.9
1978	30	People's Conference	22	37.5
		Independents	8	62.5
1979	30	People's Conference	18	32.7
		Congress (I)	5	23.9
1984	30	Congress (I)	20	40.5
		People's Conference	8	36.6
1987	30	Mizo National Front	24	43.31
		Congress (I)	13	32.99
1989	40	Congress (I)	23	34.85
		Mizo National Front	14	35.29

Year	*Total seats*	*Party*	*Seats won*	*% of votes*
		(xvii) NAGALAND		
1964	40	Independents	40	100
1969	40	Naga National Democratic Party (also known in various years as Naga National Organisation and National Convention of Nagaland)	22	38.7
		United Democratic Front (also known as United Front of Nagaland)	10	21.7
1974	60	UDF	25	30.0
		NNDP	23	35.7
1977	60	UDF	35	39.2
		Congress (I)	15	20.4
1982	60	Congress (I)	24	32.1
		NNDP	24	32.0
1987	60	Congress (I)	34	39.84
		NNDP	18	30.13
1989	60	Congress (I)	36	51.45
		Nagaland People's Conference	24	41.61
		(xviii) ORISSA		
1952	140	Congress	167	38.84
		Utkal Congress (known as Ganatantra Parishad till 1961)	31	N.A.
1957	140	Congress	56	38.21
		Utkal Congress	51	28.7
1961	140	Congress	82	43.28
		Utkal Congress	37	22.34

ASSEMBLY ELECTIONS : 1990 **PTI**

Party Position in Orissa Assembly

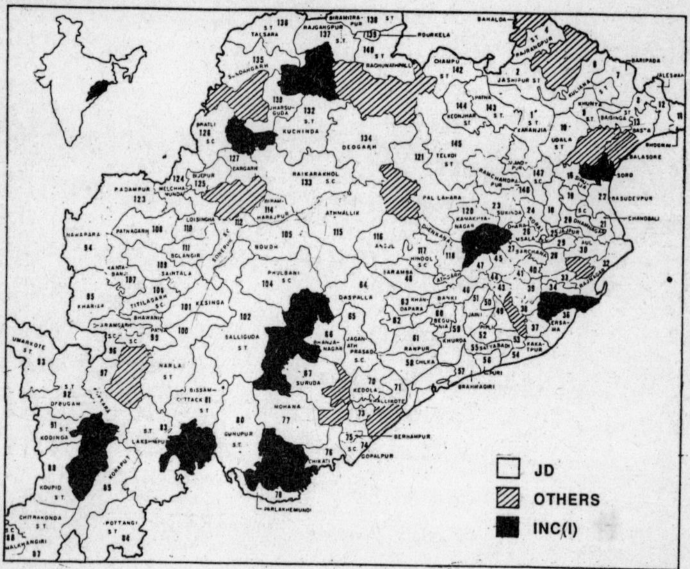

Fig. 15

Year	Total seats	Party	Seats won	% of votes
1967	140	Swatantra	49	22.58
		Congress	31	30.66
1971	140	Congress (I)	51	28.18
		Swatantra	36	17.44
1974	146	Congress (I)	69	37.44
		Utkal Congress	35	26.45
1977	147	Janata Party	110	49.17
		Congress (I)	26	31.02
1980	147	Congress (I)	118	47.78
		Janata (Secular)	13	19.49
1985	147	Congress (I)	117	51.08
		Janata Party	21	30.61
1990	147	Janata Dal	123	59.79
		Congress (I)	10	30.07

(xix) PONDICHERRY

Year	Total seats	Party	Seats won	% of votes
1964	30	Congress	21	54.3
		People's Front	4	18.2
1969	30	Dravida Munnetra Kazhagam	15	33.70
		Congress	10	42.62
1974	30	All India Anna DMK	12	27.83
		Congress (I)	7	15.84
1977	30	AIADMK	14	31.0
		Janata Party	7	26.46
1980	30	DMK	14	27.7
		Congress (I)	10	23.92
1985	30	Congress (I)	15	32.68
		AIADMK	6	15.7
1990	30	Congress (I)	11	25.05

Year	*Total seats*	*Party*	*Seats won*	*% of votes*
		DMK	9	24.06
		(xx) PUNJAB		
1967	104	Congress	48	37.7
		Akali Dal (Sant Fateh Singh group)	24	20.5
1969	104	Shiromani Akali Dal	43	29.5
		Congress	38	39.2
1972	104	Congress (I)	66	42.8
		SAD	24	27.6
1977	117	SAD	58	31.4
		Janata Party	25	15.0
1980	117	Congress (I)	63	45.2
		SAD	37	26.9
1985	117	SAD	73	38.0
		Congress (I)	32	37.9
		(xxi) RAJASTHAN		
1952	160	Congress	82	39.50
		Ram Rajya Parishad	24	N.A.
1957	176	Congress	119	45.20
		Ram Rajya Parishad	17	N.A.
1962	176	Congress (I)	88	37.58
		Swatantra (Lok Dal after 1972)	36	18.10
1967	184	Congress	89	41.42
		Swatantra	48	22.10
1972	184	Congress (I)	145	51.19
		Swatantra	11	12.32

Year	*Total seats*	*Party*	*Seats won*	*% of votes*
1977	200	Janata Party	151	50.39
		Congress (I)	41	31.49
1980	200	Congress (I)	133	42.96
		Jan Sangh	32	N.A.
1985	200	Congress (I)	113	46.56
		BJP	39	21.24
1990	200	BJP	85	N.A
		Janata Dal	54	N.A

(xxii) SIKKIM

Year	*Total seats*	*Party*	*Seats won*	*% of votes*
1979	32	Sikkim Janata Parishad	16	31.5
		Sikkim Sangram Parishad (later Sikkim Congress-R)	11	20.6
1985	32	Sikkim Congress-R	30	62.2
		Congress (I)	1	24.2
1989	32	Sikkim Sangram Parishad	32	N.A.

(xxiii) TAMIL NADU

(Known as Madras till January 1969)

Year	*Total seats*	*Party*	*Seats won*	*% of votes*
1957	205	Congress	151	45.3
		CPI	4	7.4
1962	206	Congress	139	46.1
		Dravida Munnetra Kazhagam	50	27.1
1967	234	DMK	138	40.8
		Congress	50	41.0
1971	234	DMK	184	48.6
		Congress (O)	15	35.0

Year	Total seats	Party	Seats won	% of votes
		CPM	43	18.1
1969	280	CPM	80	20.0
		Congress	55	41.3
		CPI	30	N.A.
1971	279	CPM	114	32.9
		Congress (I)	104	29.3
		CPI	13	N.A.
1972	280	Congress (I)	216	49.1
		CPI	35	8.3
		CPM	14	N.A.
1977	294	CPM	178	35.5
		Janata Party	29	20.1
		Forward Bloc	25	N.A.
		Revolutionary Socialist Party	20	N.A.
		Congress (I)	20	23.2
		CPI	2	N.A.
1982	294	CPM	174	38.5
		Congress (I)	49	35.7
		Forward Bloc	28	N.A.
		RSP	19	N.A.
		CPI	7	N.A.
1987	294	CPM	187	39.30
		Congress (I)	40	41.8
		FB	18	N.A.
		CPI	11	N.A.

(xi) 1990: A Mini General Election

Late in February 1990, three months after the formation of the new Central Government by the Janata Dal, there was a further and larger round of elections in eight States: Arunachal Pradesh, Bihar, Gujarat, Himachal Pradesh, Madhya Pradesh, Maharashtra, Orissa and Rajasthan. Elections were held also in the Union Territory of Pondicherry.

The Congress (I) had been in power in all these parts of the country, but was dislodged everywhere except in two States: Maharashtra and sparsely populated Arunachal Pradesh. The anti-Congress wave which had swept the north in November 1989 had apparently not spent itself.

A notable feature of the February 1990 elections is that the BJP did as well as it had done earlier in November 1989. It won, in round figures, nearly 500 seats out of the total of 1600 Assembly seats that were at stake. This was despite the fact that the Ramjanmabhoomi issue was no longer in the forefront, and despite a virtual breakdown of efforts at seat adjustments.

The Janata Dal, which had been the top performer among non-Congress parties in the November 1989 poll for the Lok Sabha, became the second leading party, after the BJP, in the February 1990 Assembly elections. It won nearly 450 seats out of the 1600. The Congress (I) finished third, with about 420 seats.

The Janata Dal's performance in the February 1990 elections came after, and might have been affected by, the public exhibition of factional fissures at the time of the election of the leader of its parliamentary wing on 1 December 1989. In a fast-moving and bizarre sequence, Devi Lal was elected as leader, only to decline the honour with thanks and to propose that Vishwanath Pratap Singh be elected. The party readily agreed. It was no secret that Chandra Shekhar, president of the erstwhile Janata Party which had merged in the Janata Dal, had no objection to Devi Lal becoming Prime Minister but was opposed to V.P.Singh attaining that position. The Janata Dal parliamentary party nevertheless endorsed V.P. Singh who had played the central role in organising a broad anti-Congress (I) front and leading it to victory.

Coming three months after V.P. Singh's assumption of office, the verdict in the February 1990 Assembly elections entailing an electorate of more than 215 million (upwards of 40% of the total electorate in the country) seemed to signal indirectly a confirmation of the mandate for the new Central Government in what was virtually a mini general election.

Chapter 4

Issues In– and Beyond–1989

(i) Poverty

An issue that figured in the election manifestos of all the major political parties that contested the elections to the Lok Sabha elections in November 1989 was poverty. Despite considerable increases in agricultural and industrial production since independence, poverty continues to be widespread. An international comparison of per capita Gross National Product in 161 countries, based on World Bank data as of the late 'eighties, shows India 22nd from the bottom--with only four Asian countries (Bangladesh, Bhutan, Burma and Nepal) ranking lower than India.

The manifesto of the Congress (I) listed the achievements during the five years of the Rajiv Gandhi government in these terms:

"We have achieved the highest long-term rate of growth in the economic history of post-independence India.

"We have so successfully faced up to the challenge in 1987 of one of the most severe droughts to afflict our country that, for the first time ever, the economy registered a positive rate of growth even in a year of almost unprecedented drought.

"Foodgrains production has attained a new record, as has the output of most other agricultural crops.

"All poverty alleviation programmes have been revamped and rationalized to contribute as quickly and efficiently as possible to the major national task of eradicating poverty. In the ten years that have passed since the end of Janata rule, the proportion of our population living below the poverty line has dropped from nearly a half to well under a third of the population. There is no rest for the Congress till poverty is completely eradicated.

"The Jawahar Rozgar Yojana and the Nehru Rozgar Yojana have been launched, to bring employment and the opportunity for self-employment to the doorstep of those in search of work."

The National Front's manifesto began with the words: "Appalling poverty, glaring inequality and growing destitution of large numbers have rendered India weak and demoralised." It promised to include the "right to work" in the Fundamental Rights guaranteed by the Constitution and to "evolve a set of long overdue policies for the benefit of the neglected farming community and the rural society. Not less than 50 per cent of the investible resources will be deployed for the development of rural economy."

Stating that "of all the problems facing India none is as stark as poverty", the National Front's manifesto said: "It is a national disgrace that after four decades of independence and implementation of seven five-year plans, more than two-thirds of the population remain illiterate, ill-fed, ill-clothed, ill-housed and in poor health, while the rich roll in extravagance, leading an ostentatious life...While reiterating its commitment to planning, the National Front shall use it as an instrument for widening the social base of the economy by expanding the purchasing power of the people and extending the benefit of development to the masses, rather than a small class of people."

The Bharatiya Janata Party said it "rejects both exploitative capitalism and suppressive communism... As a result of the plan priorities the country is producing more colour TV stets, but not enough steel, more computers but not enough power, more fancy cars but not enough buses, more superfine fabrics but not enough cheaper varieties of dhoties and saris. The result of this lopsided elitist sense of priorities, combined with corruption and profligacy, is that today there are more people looking for jobs than ever before, more landless farmers than ever before more, illiterates than ever before."

The CPI (M)'s manifesto characterised the five years of the Rajiv Gandhi government as "years of immense immiserisation of our people... While the prices of the common necessities of life continue to rise, the Indian peasant does not get a remunerative price for his produce. In the years of bumper harvest, food prices for the common man do not decline but continue to increase. The continuous rise in the prices of the necessities of life led to tremendous deprivation of the people, throwing millions to abject poverty and enforced starvation."

The CPI's manifesto said: "Five years of the Rajiv Gandhi government have brought the country to a sorry pass. Its economic policies have heaped more misery on the people, with 50 per cent of people forced to live below poverty line... The sugar barons have made hundreds of crores of rupees of extra profit, part of it for the Congress fund. But it is not only sugar prices that have spiralled; prices of every item of consumption of the common man have moved up in a steep manner in the last five years... There is a concerted attempt at privatisation...Planning has been downgraded, with the decision-making on projects shifted from the Planning Commission and the Yojana Bhavan to the Prime Minister's office."

(ii) Illiteracy

Article 45 of the Constitution, in the chapter on Directive Principles of State Policy, reads: "The State shall endeavour to provide, within a period of ten years from the commencement of this

Constitution, for free and compulsory education for all children until they complete the age of fourteen years."

The Constitution having come into force on 26 January 1950, the objective should have been realised by the beginning of 1960. But even at the 1981 Census the majority of the population was illiterate. The overall literacy rate for age 5 and above was 41.44, with the male literacy rate at 53.48% and female literacy rate at 28.47%. There was a marked disparity between the overall urban literacy rate of 64.89% and rural rate of 34.04%.

In addition to deploring the lack of attention to the universalisation of elementary education, the manifestos of the non-Congress parties condemned the Rajiv Gandhi government's scheme of Navodaya schools which offer, free of cost, high-quality education to children from a rural background who qualify, through a competitive entrance examination, for admission in Class VI. Considering that children from poor families either do not go to school at all or, especially girls, drop out very early, the Navodaya scheme has been viewed by its critics as a gift to the rural elite.

The Congress election manifesto says: "The New Education Policy has transformed the country's educational future, especially by making the best education in the country available through the Navodaya Vidyalayas to all boys and girls of talent, however poor their families might be or however remote the village or hamlet they inhabit."

On the other hand, the National Front's manifesto says:

"Universalisation of elementary education will receive urgent attention... The National Front believes that all children should have access to tthe same standard and type of education... The National Front government will rectify elitist aberrations in the educational system."

The BJP pledged itself to equalise educational opportunities and implement Article 45, and to "introduce compulsory moral instruction that will be non-denominational but character-building." It also promised to "promote the study of Sanskrit language as the storehouse of ancient Indian wisdom and restore its position in the three-language formula."

CPI (M) condemned "elitist education confined to narrow upper sections in accordance with the needs of the computerised industry. The elitist education policy is the reflection of social reality, of the economy at the service of the private capitalists and monopolists."

CPI said: "Rajiv Gandhi has given up the aim of cent per cent literacy and universal primary education envisaged in the Constitution. Instead he has brought a new fangled elitist educational system called Navodaya schools in which hand-picked students are given in-house education and reared as a special chosen class. If this policy continues, India will continue to be the country with the biggest illiterate population--rather a strange way of going into the 21st century!"

(iii) Corruption

Suspected kick-backs in governmental purchases from abroad--including major Defence items like the Bofors gun and the HDW submarine --figured among the allegations of corruption levelled by non-Congress parties.

On the occasion of the Congress centenary observance in Bombay on 28 December 1985, Prime Minister Rajiv Gandhi speaking in his dual capacity as Congress president had said in the course of a remarkably candid self-appraisal: "What has become of our great organisation? Millions of ordinary Congress workers throughout the country... are handicapped, for on their backs ride the brokers of power and influence, who enmesh the living body of the Congress in their net of avarice. Corruption is not only tolerated but even regarded as the hallmark of leadership." In the election manifesto of 1989, the Congress discussed the problem of corruption as one that is to be found mainly at the lower levels of administration.

The Congress manifesto said: "We must squarely tackle the problem of corruption. It is most oppressive at the grassroots, at the interface where the bulk of our people and the machinery of government meet."

The National Front said that it stood firmly "for dismantling the nexus between politicians and vested interests, and to eradicate the all-pervasive corruption. It will track down the kickback funds generated in Bofors and other deals and stashed away in foreign banks. The funds will be restored to the nation and the guilty will be punished."

The CPI (M) said: "In addition to the crimes and evils of the capitalist path, the Rajiv government has made its own contribution. No previous government of the Congress (I) was surrounded by so many corruption scandals shaking the faith of the common man in administration and the entire system... The Bofors scandal is the biggest and with the new facts coming out every day, Rajiv and his Cabinet colleagues stand tarred and condemned. Any person with the faintest attachment to parliamentary norms would have resigned. The members of the parliamentary majority in defending Rajiv Gandhi have acted as feudal retainers of the Prime Minister and betrayed the national interest for the sake of personal interest. The entire lot along with Rajiv Gandhi must be given quit orders in the elections, declaring them to be unworthy of the trust of the nation."

The CPI: "The latest revelations on the Bofors gun deal---the report of the Comptroller and Auditor General, the *Hindu* disclosures and the interview of General K. Sundarji--have dramatically shown how corruption flourishes in high places under Rajiv Gandhi's government. In fact, the finger of accusation is uncomfortably pointing to circles close to the Prime Minister himself, his having been the Defence Minister when the Bofors deal was struck. Right from the first exposure by the Swedish media up to the latest *Hindu* reports, Rajiv Gandhi's has been a stand of evasion, lies and bland denials. All this forced the opposition in the

Lok Sabha to resign in protest and seek the people's mandate."

The BJP's manifesto promised first priority for the cleansing of public life: "The party holds that the roots of all corruption lie in political corruption. The party recognises the urgency of evolving effective mechanism to break the unholy nexus between the corrupt bureaucrat, corrupt businessmen and the corrupt politician...It will enact a law and create institutions of Lokpal and Lokayukta, bringing the Prime Minister and the Chief Minister also under its purview; streamline procedures and rules relating to purchase, awarding contracts etc. in government and public sector undertakings and the discretionary powers of political authorities; and require all Ministers to make an annual declaration of assets."

(iv) Electoral Reform

The Congress manifesto takes credit for enacting, in order to bring cleanliness into politics, "two revolutionary pieces of legislation". One is the 52nd amendment of the Constitution in February 1985, popularly known as the Anti-Defection Act. It provides that if a member of parliament or a State legislature votes or abstains from voting contrary to the direction issued by the political party to which he belongs, he shall be disqualified from continuing as a member. However, if one-third or more of the members of a party break away, the Act recognises it as a party 'split'; it will not disqualify the members of the faction that breaks away. The Act precludes the jurisdiction of courts over any matter connected with the disqualification of a member.

The second legislation referred to in the Congress manifesto is the Representation of the People (Amendment) Act of 1988. It disqualifies from candidature for elections, persons who have been convicted of offences under specified sections of certain enactments. The offences covered include "undue influence or personation at an election"; inciting enmity between different groups on the ground of religion, race, place of birth, or language; bribe; or rape--all under relevant sections of the Indian Penal

Code. Other offences, conviction for which will entail disqualification, include the practice of untouchability or abetment of Sati; violation of the Foreign Exchange Act; misuse of religious premises as defined in the Religious Institutions (Prevention of Misuse) Act of 1988; and, under the Representation of the People Act, the offence of removal of ballot papers from polling stations or the offence of fraudulently defacing or fraudulently destroying any nomination paper. (Though it was claimed at the time of enactment of this amendment to the Representation of the People Act that it would keep criminals out of politics, there has been no reported case of any candidate being disqualified under the amending Act.)

In the National Front s manifesto, the section on electoral reforms says: "The Indian state cannot be rejuvenated and made to play its appointed role in social transformation unless it also steps in to combat the growing nexus between big money, mafias and the politicians. The National Front will urgently implement the long-pending proposals for publ:_ financing of elections to reduce money power, regular audit of party funds and observance by political parties of the rules framed by their respective constitutions. Contrary to the existing practice, the Election Commission will be appointed in consultation with the Opposition. System of multi-purpose photo identity cards will be introduced. Measures for expeditious disposal of election disputes, holding of bye-elections on time, and fresh delimitation will be undertaken...Suitable changes will be made in the Anti-Defection Law to prevent its misuse."

The BJP, stating that elections must be held "regularly and very fairly", pledges itself to: "Introduce compulsory voting for all citizens; arrange for public funding of elections; ban company donations; introduce identity cards for voters; use electronic voting machines in all elections; give the right of postal ballot to Indian citizens living abroad; strengthen the independence of the Election Commission by making expenditure incurred on the Commission as a charge on the Consolidated Fund of India, as is provided in the case of the Comptroller and Auditor General and the Supreme Court and High Court judges and by providing the Commission with an independent infrastructure; hold State and Central elections simultaneously every five years; examine the feasibility of introducing the List System of elections; have party accounts publicly audited; to prevent abuse of governmental power by the ruling party, give legal teeth to the Code of Conduct framed by the Election Commission, with violation of the Code made a corrupt practice under the law; empower the Election Commission to monitor all political and election coverage by Doordarshan and All India Radio and ensure that these media are not misused; and include in the limitative ceiling of election expenses all expenditure incurred by the candidate, his election agent, his party and supporters."

The manifesto of the CPI calls for: "Introduction of the system or proportional representation in elections; effective reforms in the electoral system to eliminate money and muscle power." The CPM's manifesto refers to "the falsification of Tripura elections and the establishment of a terror regime there" as an example of "the growing trend towards authoritarianism under Congress (I) rule."

(v) Secularism and Minorities

None of the major political parties questioned the need for the Indian State to be secular. But their manifestos differ on the means to be adopted. The Congress (I) and the National Front are at one in promising special measures for the progress of members of the minority religious communities, while the BJP is against promoting a 'minority complex' and the CPM stresses the need for minority masses to join hands with "the democratic and class forces" fighting injustices and inequalities.

The Congress manifesto recalls the steps taken by the Congress government "to promote the interests and fulfil the aspirations of minorities". These include the establishment of polytechnics in minority concentration areas; the benefit of special coaching schemes run by the University Grants Commission for minority community students in 20 universities and 14 degree colleges; and simplification of procedures for emigration of workers to Middle East countries. The manifesto refers to "Indiraji's 15-Point Programme" for the welfare of minorities and promises that the spread of education and development of entrepreneurship in the minority groups will be a special area of attention.

The National Front promised: "Religious minorities will enjoy the fullest protection and opportunity to pursue their modes of worship and their religious beliefs and practices, and develop their institutions--whether religious, cultural, educational or welfare-oriented. Complete non-interference will be observed in their personal laws...The Minorities Commission will be given statutory status. In order to remove unemployment and economic backwardness among the minorities, the Government would take, *inter alia,* the following steps:(i) Setting up Minorities Financial Corporations; (ii) Representation for minorities on various recruitment committees and boards; (iii) Encouragement for establishment of technical and polytechnic institutions by minorities; and (iv) Preservation of the minority character of the educational institutions guaranteed under the Constitution."

The BJP's manifesto says: "The idea of a theocratic state is an anathema to the Indian mind and the BJP believes that the State in India has always been a civil institution which respects all religions equally and makes no discrimination between one citizen and the other on the grounds of language, gender, caste or religion. It is the duty of the State to guarantee justice and security to all minorities--linguistic, religious or ethnic. The BJP considers that it is also imperative for national integration that minorities do not develop a minority complex. BJP will widen the scope of the present Minorities Commission and convert it into a Human Rights Commission to take care of the just rights of all individuals, groups and communities.

"BJP believes in positive secularism which, according to our constitution-makers, meant *Sarva Dharma Sama Bhava* and which does not connote an irreligious state. It certainly does not mean rejection of our history and cultural heritage, the very foundations of this great nation. The BJP stands for 'Justice for All and Appeasement of None'."

In its manifesto the CPI condemns "the pandering which the Rajiv Gandhi government had done to the religious fundamentalists of both sides--one side in the Shah Bano case and on the other, breaking open the locks of the Ayodhya complex." On account of this, it said, "communal forces have gained new leverage during the last few years." The CPI also flayed the BJP for campaigning "for abolition of the Minorities Commission and for scrapping of Article 370 of the Constitution."

The CPM expresses "deep sympathy with the minority Muslim masses who are the worst victims of communal fanaticism and governmental oppression during the riots. The CPI(M) at the same time calls upon the minority masses to realise that the fight for minority rights and equality to be successful has to be carried on in cooperation with the democratic and class forces who are fighting the injustices and inequities of the bourgeois-landlord rule. The bourgeios-landlord rulers are incapable of protecting the democratic rights of the minority. It is only the common fight of all sections of the masses that will deliver the minority from the injustices of the present regime. The minority communal leaders and the fundamentalists never think in terms of the common struggle of the Hindu and Muslim masses against the Congress (I) regime. They encourage and maintain the communal divisions among the masses which keep the toilers divided and help the Congress (I) regime."

(vi) Common Civil Code

Article 44 of the Constitution, in the chapter on Directive Principles of State Policy, reads: "The State shall endeavour to

aroused heated debate and even violent clashes. In the matter of job reservation, the application of quotas based on caste and tribe to promotions within a service has caused more bitterness than the reservation at initial recruitment. In the educational sphere, the reservation based on caste and tribe in institutions of professional and scientific training has caused heart-burning among students with much higher marks who fail to get admission.

The second Backward Classes Commission, appointed to review the condition of the O.B.C., was headed by B.P. Mandal and gave its report on31 December 1980. The Commission considered and rejected the suggestion of applying a means test so that the benefit of reservation goes to the truly needy. The Commission recommended that the scheme of reservation should be made applicable to public sector undertakings, both Central and State, and "all private sector undertakings which have received financial assistance from the government in one form or another", as well as to "all universities and affiliated colleges." Reservations should be applicable not only at initial recruitment but to promotions at all levels. As regards the quantum of reservation, the Mandal Commission says that, on the population criterion, OBCs--both Hindus and non-Hindus--account for 52% of the country's population and ought to have a corresponding reservation. However, "this might go against the law laid down in a number of Supreme Court judgments wherein it has been held that the total quantum of reservation should be below 50%. In view of this the proposed reservation would have to be pegged at a figure--namely 27% -- which when added to 22.5% for S.C. and S.T. remains below 50%." However, the Mandal Report says that "States which have already introduced reservation for O.B.C. exceeding 27% will remain unaffected by this recommendation." The reason is not explained, but the Mandal Commission presumably followed the example of the judgment in the Kesavanand Bharati case (April 1973) in which the Supreme Court made prospective--and not retrospective--its decision that amendments of the Constitution should not affect its basic structure.

The Congress (I) and the two Communist parties are silent in their election manifestos on the subject of the Mandal Report. The Left Front government of West Bengal is alone among the State governments in making reservations only for S.C. and S.T. The CPM-led government of West Bengal accepted the recommendation of a committee set up by it in 1980 that "poverty and low living standards rather than caste should be the most important criteria for identifying backwardness."

Application of the economic criterion in addition to caste is proposed by the BJP for reservations in favour of O.B.C. Its manifesto says: "Reservation should be continued for the S.C. and S.T. as before. Reservation should also be made for O.B.C. broadly on the basis of the Mandal Commission Report, with preference to be given to the poor among these very classes. As poverty is an important contributory factor for backwardness, reservation should also be provided for members of the other castes on the basis of their economic condition."

The National Front in its manifesto promised to implement the recommendations of the Mandal Commission expeditiously'. It says with regard to S.C., S.T. and O.B.C.: "The National Front is committed to removal of social inequality in all forms. Implementation of reservation policy will be made effective in government, public and private sector industrial undertakings, banking institutions, etc. by resorting to special recruitment drives so as to fulfil their quotas within the shortest possible time. Preferential opportunities and concessions will be ensured to Scheduled Castes even after they embrace Buddhism, in view of the fact that they continue to suffer from social disability. The socially and educationally backward classes will be given special opportunities and substantial reservations in employment, education and public offices."

(viii) Centre-State-Local Body Relations

The calling of the elections to the ninth Lok Sabha was preceded, and hastened, by the failure on 13 October 1989 of two constitutional amendments sponsored by the Rajiv Gandhi government to secure the requisite two thirds majority in the Rajya Sabha. They were intended to give rural Panchayati Raj institutions and Nagarpalikas (urbån municipalities) constitutional status and powers. While the government held that the 64th and 65th constitution amendment Bills were not intended to intrude into the jurisdiction of the States, the non-Congress parties saw in them a move to bypass State governments and establish direct Central control over local bodies.

In its election manifesto the Congress (I) gave an important place to the issue. It said: "The vast gap which at present exists between the 83 crore people of India and their 5500 representatives in Parliament and the State assemblies would have been closed by building a grassoots tier of democracy that would have brought in something like 20 lakh elected representatives, chosen by the people and responsible to them in the very same villages and mohallas where the people live. The solution to their everyday problems would have been found at a distance no further than the Panchayat Ghar or the local Ward Office of the Nagarpalika. This endeavour has been temporarily thwarted by 83 members of the Opposition in the Rajya Sabha. The Congress now takes the issue to the 83 crore people of India."

The National Front, on the other hand, characterised them as "phoney decentralisation Bills". Its manifesto said: "The National Front is committed to true federalism, and will reverse the over-centralisation brought about by the ruling party. Not only will the States benefit by decentralisation of powers from the Centre, but there will be a corresponding and simultaneous devolution of power to the districts, the talukas, tehsils, the mandals and the panchayats. The discredited attempts made by the Rajiv Government to bypass the States, through legislative measures in the name of decentralisation, will be replaced by genuine decentralisation based on a national consensus. The States ought to enjoy genuine autonomy, without the indignity of becoming supplicants before the Centre, with a begging bowl. Successive attempts have been made by the Union Government, under Rajiv Gandhi, to encroach upon the autonomy of the States."

The BJP said it would "neither impose Panchayats from above nor use them to bypass the State Government". It affirmed its commitment to genuine decentralisation: "Mahatma Gandhi and Jaya Prakash Narayan were strong votaries of local self-government. The Jana Sangh under the leadership of Pandit Deendayal Upadhyaya had always canvassed for the constitutional status of Panchayats and Municipal Boards. The party will ensure a constitutional status and assured share of resources so that they do not depend upon discretionary grants."

The CPM's manifesto said: "In West Bengal, under the Left Front Ministry, there is more decentralisation of power accompanied by more democratic and active functioning of the panchayats. This has been rendered possible because, apart from the powers given to the panchayats, the mass of peasants and agricultural workers are in a position to defeat the hold of the vested interests over the panchayats. The Panchayati Raj and Nagarpalika Bills of the Congress (I) are not genuine measures to transfer more powers to these bodies. They are an attempt to establish the overlordship of the Central Government over these institutions. They are simultaneously an attempt to erode the powers of the State governments, breaking the links between them and the panchayats. The main purpose of the amendment was to appropriate for the Centre the powers of the States."

(ix) Freedom of the Media

Prime Minister Jawaharlal Nehru said in Parliament on 15 March 1948 of All India Radio, which was being run as a government department, that "we should approximate as far as possible to the British model, the BBC. That is to say, it would be better if we had a semi-autonomous corporation." A committee established by the Government on Broadcasting and Information Media, with A.K. Chanda as chairman, recommended in April 1966 the constitution of autonomous corporations for radio as well as for Doordarshan, the Indian television system which had come up by then. The Indira Gandhi cabinet considered and rejected the recommendation. Parliament was informed in April 1970 that "it was agreed that the present is not an opportune time to consider the conversion of the All India Radio into an autonomous corporation." (Television was at that time a wing of AIR.) The Congress (I) adhered to this position until a last-minute change, incorporated in its election manifesto for the 1989 elections. The manifesto says: "The electronic media will continue to be owned by Government. However, with a view to ensuring functional autonomy, high professionalism and the right mix of entertainment, information, news and views, Akashvani and Doordarshan will be converted into corporations."

The non-Congress parties had been protesting vigorously against what they regarded as blatant misuse of the government-owned electronic media for projecting the image of the Prime Minister and of the Congress (I) and for denigrating the Opposition. Their manifestos were at one in demanding autonomy for the media and objectivity in their programmes of news and current affairs.

The National Front's manifesto said it "commits itself to full freedom of the media, autonomous corporations for television and radio, and elimination of practices that lead to direct and indirect arm-twisting of the Press. People's right to information shall be guaranteed."

The BJP said it would: "Make freedom of the Press an explicit Fundamental Right, and not just an implied one derived from the citizen's right to freedom of expression; Encourage the growth of the Press by abolishing the duty on newsprint and the tax on newspaper advertising; Revive the Prasar Bharati Bill of 1979, which sought to convert AIR and Doordarshan into an autonomous corporation, with greater autonomy than that enjoyed by BBC today; Review the Official Secrets Act insofar as it obstructs the Right to Know, and enact a Freedom of Information law; and Implement the P.C. Joshi Report on TV software, to improve the quality of TV programmes."

CPI: "The Rajiv Gandhi government has totally and shamefully abused the electronic mass media of TV and radio for partisan ends and to hurl slanders against the Opposition. This must stop. The electronic mass media must be controlled by an autonomous corporation with constant supervision by an all-party parliamentary committee."

(x) Foreign Policy

There is agreement among the major political parties that the country's foreign policy should be based on non-alignment, anti-colonialism and the promotion of peace but there are considerable differences in the perception of how these principles have been or should be applied. The sections on foreign policy in the manifestos of the parties carry sharp attacks against others.

The Congress (I) says: "Under the Congress government of Shri Rajiv Gandhi:

"The major military powers that earlier scoffed at the principles and philosophy of non-alignment are now beginning to see the world through Indian eyes.

"One of the world's great superpowers, the Soviet Union, has affirmed its adherence to the traditional Indian principle of non-violence through the Delhi Declaration signed in November 1986 between Prime Minister Rajiv Gandhi and the Soviet President, Mikhail Sergeyevich Gorbachev...In our neighbourhood, India's prestige is at a new height.

"With China, the Prime Minister's historic visit to that country in December 1988 heralded a new era of peace and cooperation between Asia's two greatest countries, not withstanding the difficult negotiations that lie ahead in resolving the border issue.

"In Pakistan, the restoration of democracy promises a new beginning. Meanwhile we remain ever vigilant in Siachen and other sensitive areas along the border.

"In Sri Lanka, the historic agreement of July 1987 has contributed to preserving the unity and integrity of Sri Lanka, while meeting our deep security concerns and ensuring the devolution of adequate political, financial and administrative powers to the Regional Councils. The genocide of the Tamils has been forestalled and democracy for the Sri Lankan Tamils ensured by protecting them from non-democratic elements within their own ranks. The noble jawans of the Indian Peace Keeping Force are to be congratulated on a difficult job extremely well done.

"There are problems with Bangladesh, many deriving from the mistakes made by the Janata Government over the augmenting and sharing of the Ganga waters, but these can be resolved with goodwill on both sides.

"With Nepal, origin of the present problem can be traced to the confused Janata regime where the then Prime Minister overruled the advice of his Foreign Minister and ordered the merging of the Treaties on Trade and Transit. A solution is being worked out.

"Our smallest neighbours, Maldives and Bhutan, are among our closest friends. Their trust in our intentions, and their goodwill towards us, give the lie to the false allegations that are sometimes made of India's hegomonistic ambitions."

On the other hand, the National Front says in its manifesto: "Our foreign policy, once lauded for defusing tensions elsewhere in the world, has now led to embittered relations even with friendly neighbours like Nepal, Bangladesh and Sri Lanka. With Nepal, negotiations will be started on all issues of contention to find an amicable solution. The National Front will help strengthen the economy of Nepal and honour her self-respect. The National Front will offer to Pakistan mutual withdrawal of visa restrictions and promotion of bilateral commerce and trade. It is in favour of discussing with Pakistan and China negotiated gradual troop reduction on the borders, leading to the lessening of tensions and the heavy burden of defence expenditure.

"The National Front shall continue the policy of refusing to sign the Non-Proliferation Treaty. It is committed to the policy of using nuclear energy for peaceful purposes only.

"The security of the nation has been gravely endangered by the Rajiv Gandhi government and made vulnerable to outside pressures. Total absence of a national security doctrine, ad hoc decision making, and easy resort to importing arms, often for extraneous considerations and kickbacks, have all adversely affected the nation's security. The National Front government will establish a National Security Council under the chairmanship of the Prime Minister. The Council will help evolve a consensus on our foreign and defence policies and coordinate with various Ministries and departments connected with national security."

BJP: "Never has the country faced so much animosity from so many of our neighbours, as today. The conduct of diplomacy by the Rajiv Government has left India's foreign policy in tatters. The BJP has stood for and is committed to mutually beneficial bilateral relations with all our neighbours and a strengthening of SAARC...Defence preparedness has suffered grievously in the hands of the Rajiv government, gripped as it is by ad-hocism and by corruption surrounding defence procurements. The other great harm that the Rajiv government has caused to the country is excessive misemployment, in an adventurous manner, of the Indian armed forces in political roles or on militarily unattainable tasks. This has caused a very serious lowering of the morale of our armed forces and hence of its total combat effectiveness. The BJP will exert for optimum defence preparedness including production of nuclear bombs and delivery systems."

CPI (M): "The U.S. imperialists with their ambition of global domination seek to bring us in the orbit of their influence, utilising our foreign borrowing, continuing internal strifes and financing anti-national elements. It is known that behind the attacks of the Khalistani terrorists in Punjab stands the training and financing of U.S. imperialists done through the military intelligence clique of Pakistan...We have been able to hold our own because of precious economic and defence help from the Soviet Union and the Socialist countries. The Indo-Soviet Treaty of Friendship and Cooperation has been the biggest support for independence in foreign affairs. The entire people of India must support and strengthen our policy of non-alignment. This is all the more necessary because the reactionary communal forces in India like the BJP and RSS denigrate this policy and in the name of genuine non-alignment demand a tilt towards U.S. imperialists. While fighting to defeat the Congress (I) the people must defeat all the attempts to destabilise our foreign policy."

CPI: "The Communist of India is proud of the role it has played in the post-independence period in strengthening India's anti-imperialist foreign policy, which has raised India's prestige in world politics. We must continue and strengthen the country's policy of peace, anti-imperialism and non-alignment, of friendship and cooperation with the Soviet Union and other countries of the Socialist world and anti-imperialist regimes; and improvement of our relations with our neighbours, including China."

Chapter 5

Psephology Arrives in India

Elections to the ninth Lok Sabha and the legislative assemblies of 14 states and the union territory of Pondicherry between November 1989 and February 1990 brought about dramatic changes in the Indian polity.

For once India's 498 million voters failed to give a decisive verdict. A minority government took shape with a "hung" parliament. The Congress was dislodged from the centre and nine other capitals, but came roaring back in the southern states of Andhra and Karnataka.

(i) Reading the Voters' Mind

But psephologists, doing with computers what their Athenian forbears did with pebbles, were not surprised. The election experts had seen it all coming. A couple of opinion pollsters just hit the bull's eye with their pre-poll predictions.

With just about fifty results in before midnight of November 26, PTI computer projections gave the Congress(I) between 190 to 200 seats in the Lok Sabha. In the event, it finished with 194 seats.

Later, a fortnight before the February 27 poll to the State Assemblies, an election expert engaged by PTI forecast that Madhya

Pradesh and Himachal Pradesh may go to Bharatiya Janata Party and Bihar and Orissa to Janata Dal, but no single party may be able to win an absolute majority in Gujarat and Rajasthan. And so it was.

How do they do it? Well, psephologists look for patterns and trends in the way Indians have voted over the last 38 years, hold opinion polls in carefully selected constituencies, and then translate the data into seats through some complex calculations based on what they call the "Cube Law", the "Index of Opposition Unity" (IOU), and the "Lying Factor".

Indian election experts have adapted the methodology evolved by Western psephologists essentially for two party systems. Several studies have shown that in such systems the seats won by a party are usually "in proportion to the cube of the percentage of votes polled by the party". By this "Cube Law" a party getting say 52 per cent of the popular vote may corner over 78 per cent of the seats and a swing of two per cent in favour of a party may give it eight per cent more seats.

In India too, one witnesses the phenomenon of the winning party getting a much larger share of seats. But notwithstanding this similarity of disproportions, the "Cube Law" in its original form does not seem to work in India. For if one treats the winning party and a combination of the losing parties as two parties, the law would give the Opposition parties a majority as the Congress, or for that matter the Janata Party in 1977, has never won the national election with the support of a majority of national voters.

But a modified version of the Cube Law seems to work in Indian type multi-party systems. This involves a marriage with another concept evolved to translate a multi-party situation into a two-party one--the concept of the Index of Opposition Unity (IOU). Psephologists Prannoy Roy and Ashok Lahiri define IOU as the proportion of votes polled by the largest opposition party to the total opposition vote. In a two party situation, the IOU would be one. A split in opposition votes would lower the IOU. Seat adjustments and understanding between various anti-Congress parties at the time of November 1989 Lok Sabha elections raised the IOU to 0.8951 which was somewhat akin to virtual one-to-one straight contests between the Congress and its opponents in nine out of every ten constituencies. By the time of February 1990 elections, the IOU had fallen to 0.7, denoting some fragmentation in the ranks of anti Congress parties and resulting in fewer straight contests.

The modified Cube Law multiplies the total vote of opposition or loser parties by the IOU and then assigns this proportion of votes to an "ideal" second party to calculate the number of seats that may be won by the losing parties together. (See Table XI at the end of this Chapter.) But even so, a review of previous election results shows that the Congress actually got more than the "predicted figure" as the "ideal" second party does not reflect the true situation on the ground (See Table XII.).

But course corrections along the way, as that for "lying factor", apparently enabled Indian psephologists to make fairly accurate predictions for the November 1989 Lok Sabha and 1990 assembly elections. An election expert says voters never tell the whole truth to opinion pollsters in regard to the way they intend to vote. But their responses to other questions can lead one nearer the truth.

Victory or defeat, however, is not wholly determined by the IOU alone and it is the "swing" and "split" factors which together spell the actual outcome of an election. Sometimes the swings and splits cancel each other out. At other times they work in the same direction to give a new complexion to electoral battles. But a study of all the elections since 1952 seems to indicate that the role of swings is more decisive. Thus Congress(I)'s second worst defeat in 1989 was brought about by a united opposition in conjunction with a drop in its popularity--from 48.1 per cent in 1984 to 39.33. The nearly nine per cent swing away from the Congress and greater opposition unity together cost Congress (I) 221 seats as its tally dropped from 415 to 194.

There was further erosion in Congress (I) popularity between November 1989 and the February 1990 assembly elections, but the split factor--as denoted by a fall in IOU from 0.8951 to 0.7--helped it retain its hold on 383 seats out of 391 assembly segments in which it had led during the Lok Sabha poll.

At the time of its last defeat in 1977, the Congress had won 154 seats on a an all-time low voter support of 34.5 per cent with 92 seats coming from the south in the elections held after Mrs Gandhi's 21 month emergency rule.

Polling an average 45.83 per cent votes the Congress had managed to corner over two thirds seats in the first three general elections in the Nehru era. But the Congress share of votes dropped to 40.8 per cent in 1967 from 44.7 per cent in 1962 and 47.8 per cent five years earlier. With 283 seats in a house of 520, Congress still had an absolute majority, but a split in 1969 reduced it to a minority.

The share of the Congress(I) as it came to be known after the 1969 split again rose to 43.7 per cent in the 1971 mid-term poll when it won 353 seats--257 of them with a more than 15 per cent margin of win.

As in 1989, the loss of about 200 seats in 1977 was not entirely due to the 9.2 per cent swing away from the Congress. Opposition Unity was decidedly a major factor. A drop in the number of candidates put up by national parties to an all time low of 1.90 per cent and a high IOU of 0.898 ensured virtual straight contests over most of the country. The result: Congress made way for the Janata at the Centre.(See Table XIII.)

But 1980 saw a reversal in the trend with swing and split factors helping the Congress to regain power. (See Table XIV.) An 8.2 per cent swing towards Congress was aided by a split in opposition ranks. The number of candidates put up by national parties per seat went up to 2.9 as the IOU dropped to 0.651. This resulted in heavy losses for the opposition whose strength went down from 388 in 1977 to 176. The Congress tally, on the other hand, went up by 200 to 353 seats won with 42.7 per cent voter support.

Experts also discern an inverse relationship between voter turnout and the performance of Congress. A higher voter turnout has generally spelt a drop in Congress votes at the national level as also the states. (See Table XV.)

But the years 1984 and 1989 appeared to be exceptions to the rule. An exceptionally high 63.6 per cent voters turned out in 1984 to give Congress its best ever win--415 seats won with a 48.1 per cent share of votes. And a drop in voter participation did not help Congress any in 1989. But 1984 was an exceptional year--with sympathy factor overriding everything else.

Indian pollsters are now looking for swing zones--or homogeneous areas which react the same way to a national swing in their voting behaviour. So far national swing zones seem to have eluded them, but one discerns interesting patterns at the state level. Feeding past patterns of electoral behaviour into computers, election experts have divided most states into at least three distinct zones. These group together traditional Congress(I) strongholds, areas which have generally voted for non-Congress parties and the constituencies which sway with electoral "winds" and "waves".

(ii) What Brings the Voter Out

A staggering 299 million voters, or nearly 60 per cent of a total electorate of 498 million, exercised their franchise in the November 1989 Lok Sabha elections. The electorate, which is larger than the combined population of Western Europe, has increased by 27.77 per cent over the last five years. About 7.71 per cent of the increase was made by over 30 million youth between the ages of 18 and 21 who were given a right to vote for the first time with the reduction of voting age to 18. As many as 49,319,722 more voters, represen-tisng an increase of 19.76 per cent over 1984, turned out at a time when countries like the United States are witnessing growing apathy of the voters. The November 1988 U.S. presidential election attracted only 50.16 per cent of the voters--down from 61.6 per cent in 1952.

Why Indian voters come out in such large numbers and why they vote the way they do is difficult to determine in a country of

A six per cent higher turnout earlier in 1967, has also been attributed in part to a concerted bid to dislodge the Congress in the first contest in the post-Nehru era. Apart from the absence of charismatic leaders, the country was going through a period of unrest in the wake of drought and resultant food shortages. The period also saw the emergence of regional parties like the DMK in Tamil Nadu and the era of coalition governments in the states. Regional parties mobilised voters in greater numbers and the villages saw a bigger spurt in turnout.

(iii) How the Indian Voter Decides

Voting for a change for the third time in nine general elections, India's 490 million electors once again confirmed that they see the battle of the hustings essentially as a contest between political parties with distinct identities.

Though political parties play an important role in the electoral process, the Indian Constitution does not anywhere refer in terms to political parties. Even the Representation of the People Act, 1951, which deals with the conduct of elections did not make any reference to political parties till 1974. Even then the reference was an indirect one in the context of leaving out the expenditure incurred by political parties from the scope of provisions relating to the filing of election expenditure by the candidates.

In spite of this, the recognition of political parties by the Election Commission became necessary in the context of reservation of symbols for the parties and the candidates put up by them.

The inclusion of a symbol for each candidate along with his name and political affiliation in the ballot paper is necessary, as noted earlier, in the Indian context where a large number of the electorate cannot read the names of the candidates and some pictorial representation is essential for the elector to enable him/her to identify the candidate of his/her choice. Accordingly the Election Commission had been specifying certain symbols as "reserved" and certain others as "free", the former being reserved for candidates sponsored by recognised political parties and the latter being equally available for all other candidates. Till the promulgation of the Election Symbols (Reservation and Allotment) Order in 1968, the criterion adopted by the Commission for recognising a political party in any State or Union Territory was that its candidates should have secured not less than 4 per cent of the total valid votes cast in that State or Union Territory either at the last general elections to the House of the People or at the general election to the Legislative Assembly. There were no separate further classifications into National, State parties, etc.

After 1968, political parties were classified into three groups: recognised national parties, recognised state parties and unrecognised registered parties. To qualify as a state party, its candidates must poll at least four per cent of the total votes cast in that State or Union Territory either in the Lok Sabha or Assembly elections. A party enjoying such support in at least four States is accorded the status of a national party throughout the country.

In all, about 200 political parties have contested the assembly or parliamentary elections at one time or another between 1952 and 1990. Many a political party has undergone several splits, mergers and changes in name. There are only two political parties which have gone through each successive electoral battle under the same symbol, name and banner--the Communist Party of India (CPI), a recognised national party and the Peasants and Workers Party (PWP), active in Maharashtra only. The Congress too has gone through several splits losing and regaining its symbol. Interestingly its current "hand" symbol once belonged to Shiromani Akali Dal, which lost it to Master Tara Singh faction of Akali Dal after a split.

At the time of the November 1989 Lok Sabha poll, there were eight National, 34 State and 251 other registered unrecognised parties.

The 1989 Lok Sabha witnessed an almost total rejection of independent candidates with only 12 of a total of 3518 candidates making it to the lower house. Among them they picked up just 5.61 per cent of the national vote and as many as 3470, or 98.6 per cent lost the Rs 500 deposit for failing to get the requisite minimum of one sixth of total votes polled in a constituency. (See Tables XVI, XVII, and XVIII)

While the share of votes polled by independents went down by two thirds from 8.42 per cent, the votes polled by National, State and Registered parties recorded an increase. The eight National parties--Congress(I), Janata Dal, CPI, CPI (M), Lok Dal, Indian Congress (Socialist), Janata Party and BJP--polled 28.4 per cent more votes than they did in 1984.

In the case of State parties like Telugu Desam, DMK, Akali Dal and the National Conference, the increase worked out at 14.06 per cent. The gains made by registered unrecognised parties like the Doordarshi Party, Bahujan Samaj Party and the Gorkha National Liberation Front totalled 8.50 per cent.

The National parties recorded a success rate of 33.77 per cent with 466 of 1380 candidates coming through. From the ranks of State parties 22.30 per cent made it to parliament with the election of 33 of 148 candidates. But only five of 569 candidates fielded by registered parties won, giving them a success rate of less than one per cent (0.88%). Thus while the voters had a wide choice--a record 6091 candidates, or just about a dozen for every seat--they were highly selective in their endorsement of credible candidates and made their choices in fairly clear cut terms.

The 1989 results again confirmed another trend--the dimimishing number of candidates who win with less than half popular support and with smaller than ten per cent margins. (See Tables XIX and XX). This is contrary to the common belief that most candidates win with small margins and on a minority vote. For instance, as many as 55.15 per cent of Congress(I)'s 194 winners came with a popular majority. In the case of Janata Dal the number of such winners formed 62.68 per cent, for BJP 61.63 per cent, for CPI (M) 65.63 per cent, and for CPI 54.55 per cent. And although only two of Telugu Desam's 34 candidates were successful, both were backed by majority votes.

Again only 8.45 per cent of Janata Dal winners had a smaller than ten per cent victory margin. BJP had 9.3 per cent such winners, Congress(I) 18.56 per cent, CPI 27.27 per cent and CPI (M) 28.13 per cent.

TABLE XXI

Percentage of candidates winning with more than 50% of votes in Lok Sabha elections

	1962	*1967*	*1971*	*1977*	*1980*	*1984*	*1989*
All-India	42.11	40.19	68.34	87.64	54.63	69.9	56.6
Southern States	35.16	64.29	89.68	89.92	81.40	79.1	65.1

TABLE XXII

Proportion of constituencies where the top two candidates polled more than 85% of votes in Lok Sabha elections

	1962	*1967*	*1971*	*1977*	*1980*	*1984*	*1989*
All India	39.7	41.0	60.9	90.0	43.4	66.3	60.2
Southern States	57.5	60.8	89.7	95.4	68.2	95.3	72.1